CAMPAIGN • 206

SPARTACUS AND THE SLAVE WAR 73–71 BC

A gladiator rebels against Rome

NIC FIELDS

ILLUSTRATED BY STEVE NOON

Series editors Marcus Cowper and Nikolai Bogdanovic

First published in 2009 by Osprey Publishing
Midland House, West Way, Botley, Oxford OX2 0PH, UK
443 Park Avenue South, New York, NY 10016, USA
E-mail: info@ospreypublishing.com

© 2009 Osprey Publishing Limited

ISBN: 978 1 84603 353 7

e-book ISBN: 978 1 84908 081 1

Editorial by Ilios Publishing Ltd, Oxford, UK (www.iliospublishing.com)
Design: The Black Spot
Index by Fineline Editorial Services
Originated by PPS Grasmere Ltd
Cartography: Bounford.com
Bird's-eye view artworks: The Black Spot

09 10 11   10 9 8 7 6 5 4 3 2 1

A CIP catalogue record for this book is available from the British Library.

ARTIST'S NOTE

Readers may care to note that the original paintings from which the colour plates in this book were prepared are available for private sale. The Publishers retain all reproduction copyright whatsoever. All enquiries should be addressed to:

Steve Noon, 50 Colchester Avenue, Penylan, Cardiff CF23 9BP, UK

The Publishers regret that they can enter into no correspondence upon this matter.

THE WOODLAND TRUST

Osprey Publishing are supporting the Woodland Trust, the UK's leading woodland conservation charity, by funding the dedication of trees.

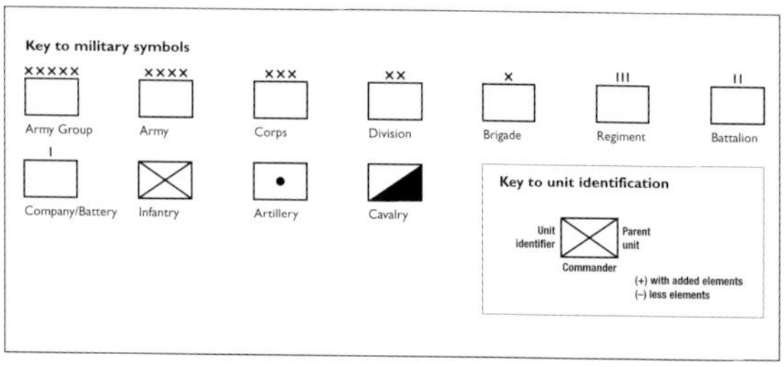

Key to military symbols

xxxxx	xxxx	xxx	xx	x	III	II
Army Group	Army	Corps	Division	Brigade	Regiment	Battalion

				Key to unit identification
I				
Company/Battery	Infantry	Artillery	Cavalry	Unit identifier — Parent unit / Commander
				(+) with added elements
				(−) less elements

FOR A CATALOGUE OF ALL BOOKS PUBLISHED BY OSPREY MILITARY AND AVIATION PLEASE CONTACT:

Osprey Direct, c/o Random House Distribution Center, 400 Hahn Road, Westminster, MD 21157
Email: uscustomerservice@ospreypublishing.com

Osprey Direct, The Book Service Ltd, Distribution Centre, Colchester Road, Frating Green, Colchester, Essex, CO7 7DW
E-mail: customerservice@ospreypublishing.com

www.ospreypublishing.com

CONTENTS

Roman province of Sicily, 75 BC

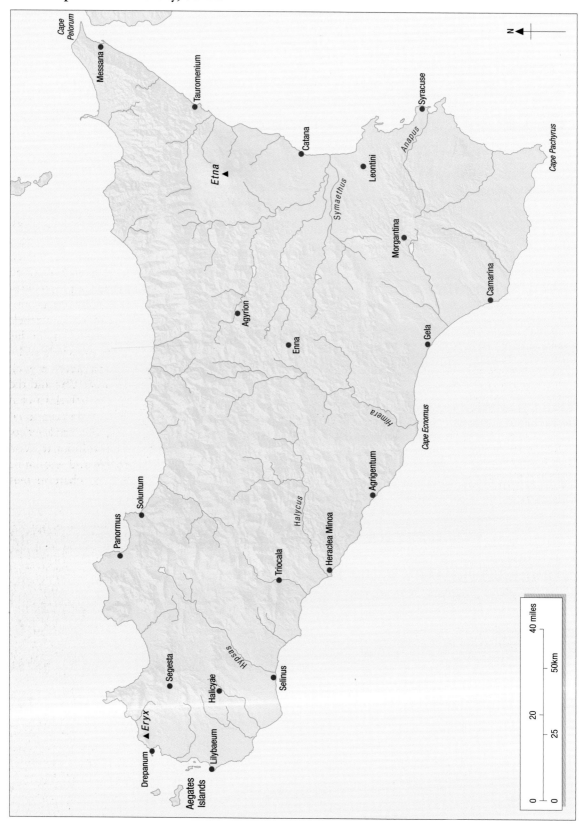

INTRODUCTION

Rocca di Cerere (left) and Castello di Lombardia (right), looking south-east outside the Eurospin supermarket, Enna. Cicero describes Enna as a town 'built on a lofty eminence, the top of which is a table-land, watered by perennial springs, and bound in every direction by precipitous cliffs' (*Verrines* 2.4.107). Besieged by Roman forces, Enna remained impregnable and only fell through betrayal from within. (Fields-Carré Collection)

The year 73 BC, the 679th from the founding of Rome, witnessed the outbreak of a serious upheaval in Italy itself, a slave-society's worst nightmare come true. This was the great slave uprising led by a charismatic gladiator named Spartacus. For the modern reader his name is synonymous with justified rebellion, the underdog daring to fight back. Not only was he the possessor in Tom Wolfe's phrase of 'the right stuff' for a Hollywood epic, Spartacus also became an important leitmotif to typify the modern wage-slave who rebels against economic exploitation and social inequality. Most noteworthy in this respect is the radical group of German Socialists founded in March 1916 by Rosa Luxemburg and Karl Liebknecht, the *Spartakusbund* (Spartacus League), who linked the Spartacus legend to protests against the Great War and the current economic order. Similarly, in more recent times, the balaclava-clad *Subcomandante* Marcos, who described himself as the international spokesperson for the indigenous rebel movement in Chiapas, southern Mexico, has used Spartacus, alongside Ernesto 'Che' Guevara, as a revolutionary icon for the popular struggle against political, judicial, social and economic inequalities, the four horsemen of an entrenched status quo, whatever that status quo may be.

Enna, a general view west-south-west from Rocca di Cerere. At the time of the First Slave War, the town was the agricultural centre of one of the richest grain-producing plains of Sicily and also an important cult centre of Demeter (Ceres), the goddess of the earth, agriculture and grain. Like the Syrian Atargatis, Demeter was a manifestation of the Great Mother. (Fields-Carré Collection)

Examples could be multiplied of Spartacus assuming a different shape according to the viewpoint of the observer: as individual hero, as leader of a significant socio-political rebellion, as potential destroyer of Rome and, of course, as inspiration for future class struggle. As it happens, we all have our own particular vision of Spartacus, be it from the perspective of political commitment or antiquarian interest. According to Plutarch, himself a Greek and one of our three main sources, Spartacus was 'much more than one would expect from his condition, most intelligent and cultured, being more like a Greek than a Thracian' (*Crassus* 8.2). The comment implies that to a Greek intellect living under the superpower of Rome, Spartacus could be considered to have overcome the natural inferiority produced by the twin handicaps of foreignness and servile status by sheer force of personality.

The historical Spartacus was rough and heroic, a big, brave and great-hearted man, and his reported actions bear out his ability to lead others and his ingenuity in battle. But like such a hero, views on his short career as a slave general oscillate between the improbabilities of fiction to the probabilities of fact. 'Spartacus', as Marx famously wrote in a letter to Engels dated 27 February 1861, 'appears to be the most capital fellow that all of ancient history can show for itself' (*Correspondence 1846–95*, 1934, p. 126). For many, this will perhaps seem like an extreme view. The revolutionary rebel Che Guevara was also a strong admirer of Spartacus. The 'Heroic *Guerrillero*' remains a well-known figure, whether adored or reviled, to millions around the modern world. As a real man, not a universal icon, he killed for a cause, ordered people to kill for that cause, advocated war to the death against imperialism, and made the ultimate sacrifice for his beliefs. Dead men may tell no tales, but they can make a legend. In the ancient world Spartacus was a real slave who rebelled, but who ultimately did not win. Yet for all this, his continued appearance on the battlefield so alarmed Rome that it mobilized a

punitive force equal to that with which Caesar was later to conquer Gaul to hunt him down and kill him.

THE ORIGINS OF THE REVOLT

The rebellion of slaves in Italy under Spartacus may have been the best organized, but it was not the first of its kind. There had been other rebellions of slaves that afflicted Rome, and we may assume that Spartacus was wise enough to profit by their mistakes. All the same, though his rebellion is easily the most famous, it is important for us to understand that stealing, petty sabotage, or simply running away, were the more usual modes of resistance employed by slaves. Full-blown wars were highly unusual.

Neighbouring Sicily, a land of various peoples, but chiefly Greeks, had become Rome's first overseas province in the wake of the first long struggle against Carthage (First Punic War, 264–241 BC). But the subsequent revival of Carthage that led to the second struggle against Rome (Second Punic War, 218–201 BC) brought a logical Carthaginian ambition to recover its former interests in Sicily and Rome in effect was forced to conquer the island anew. It was Sicily's enormous agricultural prosperity, earning it by Cicero's day the nickname 'Rome's granary' (*Verrines* 2.2.5), that was to prove the province's greatest material asset to plundering Rome.

Slavery of course was not new to Sicily, but after the Roman reconquest the scale of slave owning on the island had increased dramatically, a phenomenon Diodoros, a Sicilian himself, makes clear in his remarks (35.2.1-2, 27, 34) on the condition of the province just prior to the first great slave rebellion – the First Slave War.

Temple of Demeter (Tempio di Cerere), looking north-east from Torre Pisana, Castello di Lombardia. It was here that Eunus and his followers from the eastern Mediterranean worshipped the Great Mother in her local form as Demeter. Also it was from here, according to Cicero (*Verrines* 2.4.112), that Verres, the infamous Roman governor of Sicily, dared to take away her cult statue. (Fields-Carré Collection)

THE FIRST SLAVE WAR (135–132 BC)

Diodoros writes (35.2.4, 10) that the slaves, who had their origins in the eastern Mediterranean, motivated by their miserable living conditions and the brutality with which there were treated, had discussed rebellion before the violence actually erupted. Conveniently we can divide it into two theatres of operation, western and eastern, which reflect the basic geographical division of the island. One Roman quaestor was in charge of the western part of the island, stationed at Lilybaeum, and another was stationed at Syracuse, on the east coast. Slave herdsmen dominated the western region and agricultural slaves dominated the grain-producing plains of the east.

The slaves in the two halves of the island appear to have risen up separately – those in the east under a slave named Eunus, by birth a Syrian from Apamea, and those in the west under a herder of horses named Kleon, a Cilician from the Taurus Mountains. Eunus 'was a magician and wonder worker' with a deep devotion to the Syrian mother goddess Atargatis (Astarte), while Kleon 'had been accustomed to a life of banditry from the time he was a small child' (Diodoros 35.2.5, 3.2). It was hoped by the authorities that the two groups of rebels would come into conflict and tear each other to pieces.

Contrary to expectations, however, the rebellion gathered momentum when Kleon acknowledged the superior authority of Eunus, acting as general to his king, and their followers combined to form a single coherent force. The rapid escalation of their strength seems to have been abetted by the slave owners themselves, who had encouraged violent behaviour by allowing their slave herdsmen to feed and clothe themselves by stealing what they needed from other people on the island. In addition, the response of the local authorities was lethargic, apparently because they greatly underestimated the slaves' ability to organize a large-scale military campaign. Moreover, with more demanding overseas commitments elsewhere, a garrison army was not permanently stationed on the island.

In terms of military operations the most important officials were two consuls of Rome, and, beneath them, the six praetors. These chief magistrates were usually put in charge of Roman armies that battled formidable foreign enemies. Repressing rebellious slaves was certainly considered beneath the dignity of these men and not worthy of the talents of the legionaries they commanded. Such a sordid task was normally left to the slave owners or to local militias, which were often venal, weak, and provisional. As the permanent governing body of Rome, the Senate did have a long-term perspective on events, but it had to be moved by the recognition of a manifest threat of major proportions for it to direct the consuls or the praetors to use Roman legions to deal with a slave rebellion.

Roman provincial governors, such as those who administered Sicily, were normally former praetors who usually held their provincial commands for one-year terms. Because they were temporary and they were severely understaffed by modern standards, these governors were dependent on the great and the good that ran local towns and cities to help administer their provinces. These local landowning elites often gave their own interests priority over the rule of law and order that was supposed to be enforced by the governors. 'The Roman governors of Sicily', as Diodoros explains, 'tried to prevent the growth of these gangs, but they did not dare to punish them because of the power and influence of the landowners who were the brigands' slave masters' (35.2.2).

Given the failure of the local forces to deal with the slave rebellion in Sicily, the Senate finally decided to dispatch Roman army units to the island, first under the praetor Lucius Hypsaeus and then under two successive consuls, Lucius Calpurnius Piso (*cos.* 133 BC) and Publius Rupilius Perperna (*cos.* 132 BC). As a result, the war was finally brought to an end.

During the First Slave War, Kleon, having risen in rebellion on the western, more pastoral, side of Sicily, immediately overran Agrigentum (Agrigento), whose walls had probably fallen into disrepair, and the neighbouring region with a force said by Diodoros (35.2.17) to have numbered 5,000. Most of his followers were slave herdsmen, *pastores*. View of the south circuit of the city, looking west from the temple of Hera. (Fields-Carré Collection)

THE SECOND SLAVE WAR (104–100 BC)

To a considerable extent, the second great slave rebellion, which again erupted on Sicily, was almost a carbon copy of the first. Outlawry outside the cities and towns continued largely unaltered, not least because of the traditional association of brigandage with pastoralism. Resistance in the eastern part of the island was led by Salvius, who had the gift of prophecy, and in the west was organized by Athenion, a Cilician famous for his bravery. Athenion was not only the overseer of a large farming operation but, like Salvius, he was also reputed to possess supernatural powers, including the ability to utter prophecies based on his astrological skills (Diodoros 36.5.1). He was certainly not the ideal bailiff, called the *vilicus*, envisioned by Cato the Elder, who

Lilybaeum (Marsala) started life as a Punic city, but at its zenith it was a Roman naval base and the seat of the quaestor in charge of the western part of Sicily. Cicero would call it *civitas splendidissima*. During the Second Slave War, the rebels under Athenion felt strong enough to lay siege to Lilybaeum. This is a view of Marsala looking south-west from Isola di Mozia. (Fields-Carré Collection)

recommended among his duties that 'he should have no desire to consult diviners, augurs, fortune-tellers or astrologers' (*On Agriculture* 5.4), a ruling Columella later repeats in his agricultural treatise, adding that 'these types of silly superstition cause unsophisticated people to spend money and result in wrongdoing' (*On Agriculture* 1.8.6). Of course both he and Salvius had the capacity, in view of their ability to cast spells over their followers, to encourage the kind of resistance to authority all slave owners feared.

But there was more to leading a rebellion than the allure of mysticism. Salvius, like Eunus before him, was declared king by his followers, and he assumed the royal name of Tryphon. Intriguingly, the original Tryphon had been a barbarous, free-booting entrepreneur of violence from Cilicia, a place which became famous for its pirates, who usurped the Seleucid throne (r. 142–139/8 BC). Meanwhile in the west another slave king was proclaimed, Athenion adopting all the external trappings of monarchy, a purple robe, silver sceptre, and a royal diadem, and proclaiming to his followers that the gods intended him to rule all Sicily (Diodoros 36.4.4, 7.1, Florus *Epitome* 3.19.10). So the slave kings consciously imitated the conventions of Hellenistic kingship, the institution that had dominated the political mentality of the eastern Mediterranean world since the establishment of the Antigonid, Seleucid, and Ptolemaic dynasties. None of this should be considered unusual when we recall the fact that many of the rebels were first-generation slaves whose places of birth were in the eastern Mediterranean.

Despite the lessons of the first war, the response by the Senate was similarly slow. Its inadequate reaction, due in part to the need for Roman forces to face Germanic tribes threatening northern Italy, allowed the slaves to acquire considerable momentum in the crucial early stages of the rebellion and then to coalesce in numbers that overwhelmed the local forces trying to subdue them. Once again, the two rebel leaders came to an agreement and joined forces, with Athenion deferring to Salvius, and once again, only the intervention of the larger, better-trained and disciplined consular forces of the Roman army finally brought the war to an end.

CHRONOLOGY OF MAJOR EVENTS 146–60 BC

146 BC Romans destroy Carthage and Corinth.

138 BC Birth of Lucius Cornelius Sulla.

135 BC First Slave War begins – Lucius (?) Cornelius Lentulus, governor in Sicily, defeated.

134 BC Caius Fulvius Flaccus, as consul, sent against slaves. Uprising of 4,000 slaves crushed at Sinuessa, Campania. Slave uprisings repressed in Attic silver mines and on the island of Delos.

133 BC Tiberius Sempronius Gracchus tribune of the people – land reform and assassination. Lucius Calpurnius Piso Frugi, as consul, sent against slaves. Caius Marius serves under Publius Cornelius Scipio Aemilianus at Numantia.

132 BC Publius Rupilius Perperna, as consul, winds up First Slave War.

129 BC Marius military tribune.

125 BC Abortive bill to enfranchise Latins and Italians of Fulvius Flaccus.

123 BC Caius Sempronius Gracchus tribune of the people – socio-political reforms. Marius quaestor.

122 BC Caius Gracchus re-elected as tribune – bill to enfranchise Latins and Italians.

121 BC Caius Gracchus attempts to secure further term – outlawed and suicide.

119 BC Marius tribune of the people.

116 BC Marius praetor.

c. 115 BC Birth of Marcus Licinius Crassus.

114 BC Marius, as propraetor, governor in Hispania Ulterior – suppresses local bandits.

113 BC Cnaeus Papirius Carbo, consul, routed by Cimbri at Noreia.

111 BC Lucius Calpurnius Bestia, as consul, sent against Iugurtha of Numidia.

109 BC Marius legate under his patron, consul Quintus Caecilius Metellus, in Numidia.

107 BC Marius consul – enlists *capite censi* and returns to Numidia.

106 BC Sulla serves Marius as quaestor in Numidia – battle of the Muluccha. Births of Cnaeus Pompeius (Pompey) and Marcus Tullius Cicero.

105 BC Iugurtha captured. Consular armies routed and destroyed at Arausio.

104 BC Marius' second consulship – army 'reforms'. Insurrection of Titus Vettius Minucius, a Roman *eques* – leads an army of 3,500 slaves. Second Slave War begins.

103 BC	Marius' third consulship. Lucius Licinius Lucullus, as propraetor, sent against slaves.
102 BC	Marius' fourth consulship – Teutones and Ambrones defeated at Aquae Sextiae. Salvius (Tryphon) killed – Athenion assumes leadership of slave army.
101 BC	Marius' fifth consulship – Cimbri defeated at Vercellae. Manius Aquilius, as consul, sent against slaves.
100 BC	Marius' sixth consulship. Birth of Caius Iulius Caesar. Aquilius, as proconsul, ends Second Slave War – kills Athenion in duel.
99 BC	Marius in Asia.
98 BC	Mithridates VI Eupator of Pontus invades Cappadocia.
97 BC	Quintus Sertorius military tribune in Iberia.
96 BC	Sulla propraetor of Cilicia – installs Ariobarzanes as king of Cappadocia.
91 BC	Social War begins. Mithridates invades Cappadocia for second time.
90 BC	Enfranchisement of Italy south of the Po.
89 BC	Destruction of Asculum Picenum. Rome provokes Mithridates to war.
88 BC	Sulla consul. Mithridates overruns province of Asia. Social War ends. Sulla marches on Rome – Marius flees to Africa.
87 BC	Lucius Cornelius Cinna consul. Marius returns – Marians take Rome.
86 BC	Cinna's second consulship. Marius' seventh consulship – dies soon after. Sulla's victories at Chaironeia and Orchomenos. Birth of Caius Sallustius Crispus (Sallust).
85 BC	Cinna's third consulship. Sulla completes settlement of Asia. Sertorius praetor.
84 BC	Cinna's fourth consulship – lynched during mutiny. Peace of Dardanus.
83 BC	Sulla lands in Italy. Pompey and Crassus join Sulla.
82 BC	Battle of Porta Collina. Sulla dictator – proscription lists.
81 BC	Sulla's second dictatorship. Pompey sent against Marians in Sicily and Africa. Sertorius expelled as (pro-Marian) governor f Hispania Ulterior.
80 BC	Sulla's second consulship. Pompey's first triumph. Sertorius re-enters Iberia – establishes a Marian 'government in exile'.
79 BC	Sulla retires.
78 BC	Marcus Aemilius Lepidus consul. Publius Servilius Vatia, as proconsul, begins war against Mediterranean pirates. Death of Sulla.
77 BC	Insurrection and death of Lepidus. Pompey, with propraetorian command, sent against Sertorius.
76 BC	Successes for Sertorius in Iberia.
75 BC	Sertorius–Mithridates pact. Caesar captured by pirates.
74 BC	Lucius Licinius Lucullus, as consul, sent against Mithridates. Marcus Antonius, a praetor, given wide-ranging powers to fight pirates.
73 BC	Marcus Terentius Varro Lucullus and Caius Cassius Longinus consuls.
	Spring: gladiators escape from Capua. Occupation of Mount Vesuvius.
	Summer: Caius Claudius Glaber, as praetor, sent against slaves.

Autumn: defeat of Glaber. Publius Varinius, as praetor, sent against slave army. Defeats of Varinius and his subordinates.

Winter: slave army moves to Lucania. Crixus splits from Spartacus.

Other events: Sertorius assassinated; Caius Verres governor in Sicily; Crassus praetor.

72 BC Lucius Gellius Publicola and Cnaeus Cornelius Lentulus Clodianus consuls.

Spring: Spartacus treks northward. Defeat and death of Crixus in Apulia.

Summer: Spartacus defeats consular armies. Spartacus defeats army of Cassius. Spartacus treks southward.

Autumn: Crassus, as propraetor, sent against Spartacus. Spartacus withdraws to Bruttium.

Winter: Crassus traps Spartacus in toe of Italy. Spartacus escapes trap.

Other events: Pompey ends Sertorian War; Antonius defeated by pirates on Crete; Caesar military tribune.

71 BC Publius Cornelius Lentulus Sura and Cnaeus Aufidius Orestes consuls.

Spring: Pompey returns to Italy from Iberia. Defeat and death of Spartacus in Lucania.

Summer: Crassus' 'triumph' along Via Appia.

Winter: Pompey's second triumph. Crassus' ovation.

Other events: Antonius' humiliating peace – Senate later rejects.

70 BC Crassus and Pompey consuls. Cicero prosecutes Verres.

69 BC Lucullus invades Armenia – battle and sack of Tigranocerta. Caesar quaestor in Hispania Ulterior.

68 BC Lucullus' soldiers mutiny.

67 BC Pompey, as proconsul, sent against pirates. Mithridates defeats Romans at Zela.

66 BC Pompey, as proconsul, replaces Lucullus in east.

65 BC Crassus censor. Caesar curule aedile.

64 BC Pompey establishes Syria as province.

63 BC Cicero consul. Conspiracy of Lucius Sergius Catilina (Catiline). Caesar elected *pontifex maximus* – speaks against execution of Catilinarian conspirators. Death of Mithridates. Birth of Octavianus (Augustus).

62 BC Defeat and death of Catiline at Pistoia. Pompey returns to Rome from east. Caesar praetor.

61 BC Pompey's third triumph. Caesar, as propraetor, governor in Hispania Ulterior – victory against Lusitani. Caius Octavius' mopping-up operation in southern Italy.

60 BC The 'first triumvirate'.

ROMAN SOCIAL ORDER

Order and status, as opposed to what today we understand as class, were the vital pigeonholes for the world of Rome. Cicero, when he claims that the Senate was open to all citizens, talks of 'the highest order' (*Pro Sestio* 65.137). Thus the Romans themselves talked in the language of status groups, which entitled them to certain privileges, and if an outsider asked one of them to what class (*classis*) he or she belonged, he or she would probably refer to one of the five property classes in the oldest of the three citizen assemblies, the *comitia centuriata*. The Romans defined themselves in terms of an order (*ordo*) legally defined by the state through statutory or customary rules and in standing in a hierarchical relation to other orders (Finley 1999: 45–51). For instance Tacitus, albeit writing under the emperors, says: 'Senators and *equites* have special property qualifications, not because they differ in nature from other men, but just as they enjoy precedence in place, rank and dignity, so they should enjoy it also in these things that make for mental peace and well-being' (*Annales* 2.33.2).

Even under the emperors, when Rome was no longer an oligarchic republic, the senatorial and equestrian orders remained prestigious, a tight-knit group of families perceived to be worthy by the traditional standards of birth, wealth and moral excellence. When Cicero claims that the highest order, to which senators belong, is an open one, the last thing he had in mind was opening the doors of the Senate to those at the other end of the social scale. In Cicero's Rome 'money talks' and all men have a price. Indeed Ovid, one of the Augustan poets, laments the fact that the 'Senate is barred to the poor' (*Amores* 3.8.55). In a similar vein Horace (*Epistulae* 1.1.58), a contemporary of Ovid, wrote unhappily that 400,000 *sestertii*, the appropriate amount of property to be registered as an *eques* at the census, opens the way to the honours of Rome.

In the meantime the lower orders in Rome were a vast amoebic body, vague and murmuring. To most of us what is more invidious are the views held by that darling of classicists through the ages, Cicero. He wrote in a pungent style and never failed to flay the city-dwelling commoners, the Roman *proletarii* who huddled together in tottering tenements built not for people but for moles, often referring to them, amongst other things, as 'the city scum' (e.g. *Epistulae ad Atticum* 1.19.4). He acknowledges the grinding poverty and social misery they have to endure, but, to add insult to injury, as it were, he sees it as their own fault, blithely using the word *egens*, destitute, for the poor and even goes so far as to mention 'the destitute and felonious' (*egens et improbus*, *De domo sua* 89) in the same breath. Little did Cicero appreciate that for the proletariat of Rome, buried in a monochrome life without prospects, the furthest horizon had always been tomorrow. But what of those beneath the social pile, that is, those of servile status?

THE SLAVE SYSTEM

Slavery is an aspect of antiquity that is highly controversial. It remains an emotive subject even in the 21st century, especially as slavery was a facet of western civilization that has raised a massive amount of debate but nevertheless has played an important, albeit grievous, part in our own economical and social history.

In the literature of Rome slaves are ever present, and, for instance, the agricultural writers Marcus Porcius Cato (237–149 BC), known also as the Elder to distinguish him from his great-grandson, and Marcus Terentius Varro (116–27 BC) both presume that the main labour element was the alien slave. We also find slaves in workshops and commercial operations, but it would be wrong of us to assume that the largest concentration of servile labour was involved in productive work, especially on landed estates. As a matter of fact, the biggest concentration of slaves was in households, where they performed non-productive duties as domestics. Roman law made a clear distinction between *mancipia rustica* and *mancipia urbana* (including those in the *villa rustica* or farmhouse), the latter slaves being those with which the head of the household surrounds himself for the sole purpose of his lifestyle, *sua cultus causa*.

Almost immediately the question arises: was Roman society a slave society? Statistically, slavery was not that prevalent in the Roman world and large tracts of the empire were left untouched by servile labour. However, we cannot answer this question by statistics alone. Roman society was a slave society simply because slavery as an institution dominated the Roman mentality. After all, *libertas*, freedom, was defined as not being enslaved.

Those who worked in the fields, mills and mines were subject to an existence of hard, backbreaking labour. In his novel, *The Golden Ass*, the African Apuleius offers an uncompromising glimpse of the crushing condition of slaves working in a flour mill:

> Their skins were seamed all over with the marks of old floggings, as you could see through the holes in their ragged shirts that shaded rather than covered their scarred backs; but some wore only loin-cloths. They had letters marked on their foreheads, and half-shaved heads and irons on their leg. (*The Golden Ass*, 9.12)

These hapless souls had to trudge round and round the millstone in unending circles, their feet weighed down in irons. To make them walk their circles quicker, their backs would be stung with a lash. Gradually their eyes would grow sightless with all the dust and dark.

The owner of slaves enjoyed complete power over them, even that of life and death. A horrifying inscription (*AE* 1971.88) from the seaport of Puteoli appears at first to be nothing more iniquitous than a labour contract (*manceps*) for the public undertaker of that said town, laying down his hours of work and rates of pay. However, on closer inspection the reader will see that one of the undertaker's duties is that of 'friendly neighbourhood slave torturer'; a list of prices is given for various nasty deeds ranging from scourging to crucifixion (column II, lines 8–14).

There were good and bad slave owners, but this was a matter of pure chance. Roman society had an ingrained mental attitude to slaves, a society where man commanded, woman bore, and the slave laboured, for such was

Agora of the Italians, Delos. It is possible that this was a slave market, built as a result of the First Slave War. A generation before the Romans had made Apollo's sacred island into a free port exempt from taxes and soon Delos acquired the grim reputation of being the slave market *par excellence*, boasting that it could handle 10,000 slaves a day. (Ancient Art & Architecture)

the Roman order of things. Indeed, in the eyes of Roman law a slave was not a person but *res*, a thing subject to the dominion of his or her master. We must be careful here, however, as there was no suggestion that the Romans themselves considered a slave more as a thing than a person, and the condition that puts one individual at the mercy of another had to be regulated, the censors, for instance, being empowered to check unwarranted acts of violence upon slaves. The term *res* implies that a slave had no rights, *pronullo*, but duties, and this legal definition separated him or her from other forms of subordination. In his handbook on agricultural practices Varro, Spartacus' Roman contemporary, emphasizes that the bailiff, the *vilicus*, should not employ whips when words will suffice (*On Agriculture* 1.17.5). Athenaios perhaps expresses it best when he explains the principle of servile divide and rule, exploring the tension between an owner's rights over a slave and the uneasiness over an owner who was excessively cruel:

> There are two safeguards that one may take: first, those who are going to be slaves must not come from the same country of origin, and in so far as it can be arranged they must not speak the same language; and secondly, they must be properly looked after – and not just for their sakes; anyone who wishes to pay proper regard to his own interests should never behave arrogantly towards his slaves. (Athenaios 6.265a)

Slaves were certainly human beings, yet to cow them into the necessary docility of a brute beast necessitated a regime of calculated brutality and terrorism, especially so on farms, where *vilici* exploited the strength of slaves. More than a hundred years after the Spartacan rebellion had been crushed, the senator and philosopher Seneca formulated the most liberal set of doctrines on slavery that had been articulated at Rome. Advocating that masters should treat their slaves with lenience, Seneca broke down the artificial distinction between slave and free and insisted that all men shared a common origin and a common morality, a spiritual brotherhood of mankind if you will.

In *De beneficiis* (3.18-28) he poses the question whether or not it was possible for a slave to benefit his master. Before answering, Seneca makes an interesting distinction about terms: a) *beneficum*, a good deed or favour performed as a free and voluntary gesture by an individual under no obligation to the recipient; b) *officium*, a duty performed by a son, daughter, wife, etcetera, towards a father, husband, head of household, patron, etcetera, namely an obligation of duty; and c) *ministerium*, an action expected from a slave as he or she has no other choice but to perform this action. Seneca then cuts to the chase by saying that it is not the social standing, which was simply an accident of birth, but the intention of that individual bestowing the favour, duty or whatever. Nevertheless, a counterargument runs as follows: a slave cannot be accountable to the master if he or she gives money or tends him when ill, but Seneca immediately ripostes by saying he was thinking of the slave who fights for the master or refuses to reveal his secrets even under torture. It is a mistake, explains Seneca, to believe that a slave's mind is not free even if his or her body is owned.

Another fascinating passage is to be found in one of Seneca's *Moral Letters* (*Epistulae Morales* 47), written after his retirement from public life. Here the philosopher asks a friend if he is on good terms with his slaves, and naturally the friend replies in the affirmative. Seneca then points out that they are still slaves, to which the friend replies yes, but human beings all the same. Again Seneca points out they are still slaves, and so on and so forth. And then Seneca makes a lunge with the Roman proverb 'so many slaves, so many enemies' (*quot servi, tot hostes*, 47.5), that is to say, your enemies are the people working for you. The rule of fear may have been the basis of the master–slave relationship, but one might riposte, as Seneca does here, that such fear bred a savage cruelty in the masters and thus 'we turn them into enemies'.

Of course all this moral posturing came out of a Stoic, and nowhere in his vast corpus of writings does Seneca actually call for an abolition of slavery. On the contrary, Stoicism, the dominant school of philosophy since the late Republic, promoted the belief that what did not affect the inner man was an irrelevance. So war, which was a disturbance of cosmic harmony, caused by man's wickedness or wrong judgement, and its horrors, such as death and enslavement, were irrelevant to a good man. Thus was the Stoic a free man, having chosen to be free. It was argued that it was impossible to enslave a man against his will – he had to consent to be a slave, otherwise he might choose to die a free man. The goal was progress, not perfection.

In Caius' *Institutiones*, an introduction to Roman jurisprudence written around AD 161, we find a legal definition of slavery: 'the state that is

Relief (Mainz, Mittelrheinisches Landesmuseum) decorating a column base from the *principia* of Mainz-Mogontiacum showing two naked captives chained together at the neck. It is conceivable that they are Gauls, since their horse's mane hairstyle indicates the Celtic practice of washing it in chalky water and then combing it back from the forehead to the nape. This was probably done to enhance fearsomeness on the battlefield. (Ancient Art & Architecture)

recognized by *ius gentium* in which someone is subject to the dominion of another person contrary to nature' (1.3.2). The *ius gentium* was a law on the customs and practices found in all known peoples and not an international legal code as such. But why contrary to nature? Because, as Caius reasons, the state of freedom is what is natural even if people are born slaves. In other words, slavery is a human invention and not found in nature. Indeed, it was that other human invention, war, which provided the bulk of slaves, but they were also the bounty of piracy (e.g. Strabo 14.5) or the product of breeding (e.g. Columella *On Agriculture* 1.8.19).

It has always been assumed that the sturdy peasant-farmer worked the land for himself and his family. The Greek poet Hesiod, a small-scale farmer himself, tells us that the three vital things needed by a farmer 'are a house, a wife and a ploughing-ox' (*Works and Days* 405). Naturally, in the homely parsimony of Hesiod, the wife serves as another source of labour power, but at what point do we witness landowners resorting to slave labour?

Undeniably, there was a huge influx of slaves into the Italian peninsula following Rome's successful expansionist wars. Equally, some of the figures in the table below of those carried off to the Roman slave market, given by the ancient authors for the second century BC, are impressive and daunting:

Date	Ethnicity	Source
177 BC	5,632 Istrians	Livy 41.11.8
167 BC	150,000 Epeirotes	Livy 45.34.5
146 BC	55,000 Carthaginians	Orosius 4.23.3
142 BC	9,500 Iberians	Appian *Iberica* 68
101 BC	60,000 Cimbri	Plutarch *Marius* 27.5

Of course, cliometrics have limited application for antiquity, as ancient authors cited numbers symbolically not statistically. Nevertheless, it has been estimated that at the end of first century BC the body of slaves in Italy amounted to between two and three million people out of a total of six to seven-and-a-half million (including Gallia Cisalpina), or roughly one-third of the population (Brunt 1971: 124, Hopkins 1978: 102). But did this massive import of slaves have serious repercussions on the organization of agricultural labour in the peninsula?

Strange as it may appear, it can be argued that slavery is not the obvious method with which to exploit the land. Agricultural work is seasonal work, but slave labour has to be kept and fed all year round. It has now been recognized that a lot more free labour was working the land in Italy (Garnsey–Saller 1987: 75–77). Aristocratic landowners could, and did, divide their land into plots and rent them out to tenant peasant-farmers, who in turn managed the tenancy with the help of their own families or even that of seasonal hired labour. In fact, the tenant peasant-farmer had always been part of the agricultural scene and he was a viable alternative to slave labour even in the second and first centuries BC. As already noted, both Cato and Varro assume in their agricultural treatises that slaves will form the core of the permanent, brute labour force on the farm (e.g. Cato *On Agriculture* 2.2-7, 5.1-5). However, they were writing for a particular milieu, the senatorial landowner with a landed estate that was plugged into an international market of surpluses, a man like Cicero (*De officiis* 1.151), who praises agriculture both as a source of wealth and on moral grounds. For these big men of vast means was there 'any land', in the rhetorical words of Varro, 'more fully cultivated than Italy?' (*On Agriculture* 1.2.3).

So investment farming, as opposed to the prevailing practice of subsistence agriculture, was only really applicable to the narrow coastal lands of central and southern Italy and the island of Sicily. Here a few wealthy landowners held land in the form of huge tracts of arable-cum-pasture-land, the *latifundia* or 'wide fields' of Roman literature, where large slave populations were found in three areas: a) viticulture and olive growing; b) livestock raising; and c) cereal production.

This leads us on to a discussion of Rome as a 'slave economy'. There are a number of ways of looking at this issue. We could argue that a slave economy only existed when the majority of those involved in that society's economy were slaves, but in that case there has never been such an economy. Even the Deep South of the pre-Civil War United States did not meet this criterion. Much more productive is the notion that a slave economy is one in which the dominant mode of production sets the pace for the rest, that is, slave production or not. Thus slaves were a major engine of the economy of the Deep South, as they were of those of classical Greece, the Hellenistic east and Rome. In other words, not everybody owned slaves but if the money was available everybody would buy slaves, with the slave-run estate being seen as the ideal. Of course an economy could exist without the institution of slavery. If we look forward into the late Roman world we witness another form of subordinate labour arising in which free men were tied to the land, that is to say, the institution of feudalism, which served to produce a surplus so as to allow an elite group to exist.

We should also consider the actual cost of a slave. According to Plutarch, the elder Cato 'never once bought a slave for more than 1,500 *drachmae*, since he did not want luxurious or beautiful ones, but hard workers, like herdsmen' (*Cato major* 4.4, cf. 21.1). The *drachma* was the Greek equivalent of the Roman *denarius*, which must have been the term Cato himself used. Since at this time (it was to be retariffed at 16 to the *denarius* at the time of Gracchi) there were 10 *asses* to the *denarius*, the sum of 1,500 *drachmae* was equivalent to 15,000 *asses*. Compare this with the legionary *stipendium*, allowance, which in Cato's day was five *asses* per day (to cover rations, clothing, and repairs to arms and equipment). So the cost of an agricultural slave might equal 3,000 days' worth of *stipendium*. So slaves were not cheap, even at the height of the wars of conquest.

According to his own testimony Cato (*On Agriculture* 10.1, 11.1) reckoned an olive grove of 240 *iugera* (*c.* 60ha) should be worked by 13 slaves, and a vineyard of 100 *iugera* (*c.* 25ha) worked by 16 slaves, and Varro (*On Agriculture* 1.18), after discussing the limitations of Cato's mathematics, basically agrees with him. One slave alone must have been a considerable prize for a legionary in war. Thus the fact that slave numbers were huge does not allow valid deductions to be made about the greater or lesser availability of slaves in the population as a result of warfare, about the proportion of slaves in the population as a whole, or about the proportion of citizens who owned slaves – they are rather a sign of the increasing concentration of wealth in a small number of particular households.

In *The Banqueting Sophists* (*Deipnosophistae*), an enormous compendium of the conversations of philosophers at a banquet supposedly held in Alexandria around the year AD 200, Athenaios upholds the myth that the virtuous Romans of old, nobles such as Scipio and Caesar, owned a mere handful of slaves (6.273a-b). However, he does acknowledge that some Roman slave-holdings were extravagantly large. Yet clearly Athenaios thought that the purpose

Relief (Rome, MNR Palazzo Massimo Alle Terme, inv. 126119) depicting 'Samnites' in the arena, dated *c.* 30–10 BC. Each is armed with a *gladius* and carries a *scutum*, and appears to wear one greave on the left or leading leg. A triangular loincloth is tied about the waist, pulled up between the legs and tucked under the knot at the front and secured by a broad belt. (Fields-Carré Collection)

of owning such vast numbers of slaves was primarily to demonstrate one's wealth, and since wealth was linked to status, it could be advertised through conspicuous consumption (6.272e, 273c). This was not only true of Romans. Antiochos IV, for instance, sought to impress his subjects by organizing a procession involving hundreds if not thousands of slaves (Polybios 30.25.17), and it was a mark of extreme indignity for the exiled Ptolemy VI to arrive at Rome accompanied by just four slaves (Diodoros 31.18.1-3). But then again, these men were kings. Caius Caecilius Isidorus, a Roman landowner who flourished in the generation following the Spartacan rebellion and who himself was a former slave, had come to own 3,600 pairs of oxen, 257,000 other livestock and 4,116 slaves at the time of his death in 8 BC (Pliny *Historia Naturalis* 33.135).

PIRACY AND THE SLAVE TRADE

When strong kingdoms with powerful navies existed, such as those of the Hellenistic kings, piracy was usually reduced to a minimum. Yet the last hundred years of the Roman Republic saw one of the most remarkable developments of piracy that the Mediterranean has known, when from mere freebooters the pirates organized themselves into a pirate-state with headquarters in Cilicia and Crete. It was the more remarkable that the sea was controlled by a single power, which, when it put forth its strength under a capable leader, had no difficulty in putting an end to a malignancy in such a short space of time. The ease with which Pompey finally achieved its suppression has naturally led to a severe condemnation of Rome's negligence and apathy in permitting piracy to flourish for so long a period. This is especially so when the alliance formed between Mithridates and the pirates of Cilicia had given the Pontic king command of the Aegean, which had been nearly fatal to Sulla (First Mithridatic War, 89–85 BC).

This was partly due to the turmoil of the times, which hindered policing of the seas, and partly due to the influence of Roman slave dealers who tolerated the pirates as wholesale purveyors of slaves. The more that the economy was glutted with slaves, the more dependent it became on them. Whether conveying victims of war or those of kidnapping, there can be no doubt about the important role played by pirates in maintaining the level of the Roman slave supply, directing their human cargoes to destinations such as Sicily where they were needed. The pirates were the most consistent suppliers. Appian writes that the pirates operated 'in squadrons under pirate chiefs, who were like generals of an army' (*Mithridatica* 92). At this level of organization they were capable of raiding roads and besieging towns along the coasts of Italy. They even staged predatory raids into the western Mediterranean, where they were reputed to be in contact with various insurgent movements, including Sertorius in Iberia and, as we shall see later, Spartacus in Italy.

GLADIATORS – MEN OF THE SWORD

When Perusia (Perugia) capitulated to Octavianus and the survivors were rounded up, he allegedly took 300 rebel senators and *equites* and, in the words of Suetonius, 'offered them on the Ides of March at the altar of Divus Iulius, as human sacrifices' (*Divus Augustus* 15.1). Not long afterwards, Octavianus

having metamorphosed into Augustus, Virgil has the emperor's legendary ancestor, the pious Aeneas, perform human sacrifice at the funeral of the young prince Pallas:

> Then came the captives, whose hands he had bound behind their backs to send them as offerings to the shades of the dead and sprinkle the funeral pyre with the blood of their sacrifice. (Virgil, *Aeneid* 11.81–84 West)

Historically it was the Etruscans, a people regulated by a highly ritualized religion, who made it their custom to sacrifice prisoners of war to the shades of their own fallen warriors. Livy says that in 358 *bc* a total of 307 Roman soldiers were taken prisoner and slaughtered as human sacrifice in the forum of the Etruscan city of Tarquinii (Tarquinia); in revenge 358 captives, chosen from the noblest families of Tarquinii, were dispatched to Rome three years later and publicly flogged in the Forum and then beheaded (7.15.10, 19.2-3). The Tarquinienses may have been enacting a form of human sacrifice, but the Roman response – if historical – was an act of vengeance, not cultic obligation.

So gladiators perhaps originated from such Etruscan holocausts in honour of the dead: they were sometimes known as *bustuarii*, funeral men, and the contest was called a *munus* from being a duty paid to the deceased by his descendants. The African Christian Tertullian, writing around AD 200, describes these combats of the amphitheatre as the most famous, the most popular spectacle of all:

Funerary painting from Paestum (Gaudo Tomb 7 North Slab, *c.* 340 BC) depicting a duel. Such paintings were not mere decorative elements, as they reflect the values and ideals of the Lucanians who now controlled Paestum. This scene represents the final moments of a competition, with a judge standing behind the winner about to place a wreath on his head. These duels were not to the death. (Fields-Carré Collection)

Crucial to the development of the spectacle of gladiatorial combat were the *lanistae*. They were indispensable operators who functioned as slave traders, managers, trainers, and impresarios all in one. However, they were seen by their fellow citizens as utterly contemptible, some think like an unpleasant cross between a butcher and a pimp. Sculptural relief (Selçuk, Arkeoloji Müzesi) showing a *lanista* armed with baton and shield. (Fields-Carré Collection)

The ancients thought that by this sort of spectacle they rendered a service to the dead, after they had tempered it with a more cultured form of cruelty. For of old, in the belief that the souls of the dead are propitiated with human blood, they used at funerals to sacrifice captives or slaves of poor quality. Afterwards, it seemed good to obscure their impiety by making it a pleasure. So after the persons procured had been trained in such arms as they then had and as best they might – their training was to learn to be killed! – they then did them to death on the appointed day at the tombs. So they found comfort for death in murder. (Tertullian *De spectaculis* 12)

So Rome turned *munus*, in the fiery anti-pagan eloquence of Tertullian, into a 'pleasure' and a 'more cultured form of cruelty'. As well as punishment and sacrifices, *munera* became public entertainment.

Alternatively, 4th-century tomb paintings and vase paintings from Campania seem more obviously to depict armed single combats, and literary sources do refer to Campanian combats at banquets (e.g. Strabo 5.4.13, Athenaios 4.153f-154a). In these Campanian combats elite volunteers competed for prizes, fighting only to the point of first bloodshed. The Romans became familiar with Campanian gladiatorial combats at the tail end of the same century. Livy speaks of a battle in 308 BC of Romans and Campanians against the Samnites, who fought with inlaid shields, plumed helmets, and greaves on the left leg. As they advanced into battle, the Samnites 'dedicated themselves in the Samnite manner' while the Roman commander, who was posted on the left wing, met them head-on 'declaring that he offered these men as a sacrifice to Orcus' (Livy 9.40.12). Celebrating the victory, the Romans adorned the Forum with captured arms: 'Thus the Romans made use of the splendid arms of their enemies to do honour to the gods; while the Campanians in their pride, out of hatred to the Samnites, equipped the gladiators who provided entertainment at their banquets with similar armour and gave them the name of Samnites' (ibid. 9.40.17).

Whatever its true origins, the first gladiatorial fight took place in Rome in 264 BC, the year when the first war with Carthage began. At the funeral of Decimus Iunius Brutus Scaeva his two sons, Marcus and Decimus Brutus, for the first time exhibited, in the market called Forum Boarium, three simultaneous gladiatorial fights. It may have been a modest affair by later standards, but half of Rome apparently turned out to watch the fight. The following statistics show how fast the idea caught on

Date	Numbers	Source
264 BC	3 pairs of gladiators	Valerius Maximus 2.4.7
216 BC	22 pairs of gladiators	Livy 23.30.15
200 BC	25 pairs of gladiators	Livy 31.50.4
183 BC	60 pairs of gladiators	Livy 39.46.2
174 BC	74 pairs of gladiators	Livy 41.28.11

Initially, gladiator duels took place in whatever public spaces a town might possess. Under the emperors, however, the characteristic scene for such displays was the amphitheatre. The first known permanent amphitheatre is not in Rome but Pompeii (c. 70 BC), an enormous structure for a provincial town with its seating capacity of 20,000 places. A view of the amphitheatre looking north-west with Vesuvius in the distance. (Fields-Carré Collection)

Beginning as a grandiosity occasionally added to an aristocratic funeral, the gladiators themselves being taken from amongst the personal slaves of the deceased and equipped in makeshift fashion, over time the combats were extended to public celebrations. And so it was by Cicero's day the masses, as he says (*Pro Sestio* 106, 124), could express themselves at assemblies, elections, games (*ludi*) and gladiatorial contests (*munera*).

In 105 BC, for the first time, the two consuls of the year gave a gladiatorial spectacle officially. Indeed, one of them, Publius Rutilius Rufus, began the practice of employing gladiatorial trainers to instruct new army recruits (Valerius Maximus 2.3.2). It soon became customary for gladiatorial displays to be put on not only by victorious generals, as a feature of their triumphs, but also by officials of every rank. Such spectacles, obviously but not solely, were political devices used by Roman aristocrats to gain support. The functionaries known as aediles, for example, sought to attract popularity by giving *ludi honorarii*, supplementary games attached to theatre and circus performances.

It was as one of the aediles of 65 BC that Caesar, in memory of his long-dead father, gave a magnificent gladiatorial spectacle. However, at a time when the memory of the Spartacan rebellion must have been still fresh in people's mind, he 'had collected so immense a troop of combatants that his terrified political opponents rushed a bill through the Senate, limiting the number that anyone might keep in Rome; consequently far fewer pairs fought than had been advertised' (Suetonius *Divus Iulius* 10.2). Caesar was undaunted. He made certain everyone in Rome knew that it was the Senate that had robbed them of the most spectacular games of all time. All the same his diminished troupe of gladiators still amounted to 320 pairs, and each man was equipped with armour specially made from solid silver.

In 1874 Raffaello Giovagnoli (1838–1915), who had fought with Garibaldi, published his epic novel *Spartaco*. The comparison between ancient and modern is made explicit by the author, and Garibaldi himself wrote the preface. The illustrations were executed by Nicola Sanesi, and here we see Spartacus, brave yet compassionate, sparing the life of his friend Crixus in the arena. (Reproduced from R. Giovagnoli, *Spartaco*, Rome, 1874)

It was from successive waves of prisoners of war conscripted as gladiators that the profession was to inherit its bizarre, exotic uniforms, which was one of the sources of public enjoyment. From Rome's brutal wars of expansion during the second and first centuries BC, which eliminated most of its serious competitors for power, there was a ready supply of foreigners who had suffered the fate of slavery through capture in warfare. These were tribal warriors or trained soldiers who could be pushed into the arena with little need for preparation, being made to fight with their native weapons and in their ethnic styles. Many of these men, it is true, were simply wretched captives herded before the baying, blood-maddened spectators, but various classes of professional gladiator likewise came from this category, especially the war hardened. These earliest trained killers appeared in the arena as prisoners taken during the war with the Italian allies, the Social War, as it is generally called, of 91–88 BC, and were chiefly from the Samnites of central eastern Italy, dressed in the heavy, resplendent armour of the Samnite warrior. Soon after the Samnites, Gauls started to appear in the arena. Again these were originally prisoners of war taken from the tribes of Gaul. By about the early seventies BC these two had been joined by a third type of gladiator based on another foreign foe, the Thracian.

Cicero's metaphorical use of gladiatorial retirement in the *Second Philippic* (29) is the first known reference to awarding the *rudis* or wooden sword of freedom, the clear implication being that by his day gladiators were an investment, skilled artisans to be rewarded and not wasted. For what it is worth, Florus reckons the excessive size of gladiatorial troupes led to the Spartacan rebellion:

> How else could those armies of gladiators have risen against their masters, save that a profuse expenditure, which aimed at winning the common people by indulging their love of shows, had turned what was originally a method of punishing enemies into a competition of skill? (Florus *Epitome* 3.12.10).

Yet it was not until the early years of the Principate that there would be the many categories of gladiators that we are more familiar with, namely gladiators who were distinguished by the kind of armour they wore, the weapons they used, and their style of fighting. And so when Spartacus was a gladiator, *munera* were still in the process of becoming a prolific form of popular entertainment, and the elaborate protocols of combat and spectacle known to history had yet to be developed.

OSCAN SPEAKERS

In the central section of the Apennine chain, which forms the spine of the Italian peninsula, most of the Italic peoples spoke a language called Oscan. This was a tongue closely related to Latin, but had some distinctive characteristics. The Oscan speakers were divided into various groupings; the most important of which were the warlike Samnites who inhabited the mountainous region due east of Rome down to the area behind Campania. At the time of their long, hard wars with the Romans in the fourth and third centuries BC the Samnites consisted of four main groups, each with its own territory: the Carricini, Caudini, Hirpini, and Pentri, to whom we should probably add the Frentani. But these Oscan groups often formed new tribal configurations. In the late 5th century BC a new Oscan-speaking people, the Lucanians (Lucani), emerged (perhaps a southern offshoot from the Samnites), and in the middle of the following century another Oscan-speaking people, the Bruttians (Bruttii), split off from the Lucanians in the toe of Italy.

The instability of these Oscan-speaking peoples was probably the product of population pressure. Good arable land was in particularly short supply in the upland valleys of the Apennines, and in the course of the 5th and 4th centuries BC the highlander warriors made frequent incursions against coastal settlements, many of them founded by Greeks. So the Samnites conquered Greek Cumae and Etruscan Capua, merging with the existing inhabitants of Campania and becoming known as the Campanians (Campani). Meanwhile the Lucanians overran Poseidonia, renaming it Paestum but maintaining the

Triple-disc cuirass and Attic-style helmet with impressive iron three-branched crest-cum-feather-holder, Paestum (Gaudo Tomb174, *c.* 390/80 BC). This elaborate style of armour was peculiar to Oscan-speaking warriors, and a broad bronze belt, the symbol of manhood, would normally accompany it. Thus for a time the Romans regarded, in the sporting language of their arena, 'gladiator' and 'Samnite' as synonymous terms. (Fields-Carré Collection)

socio-political institutions set up by the Greek colonists, and attacked other Greek cities on the south-east coast. Naturally their warrior ethic encouraged wars of conquest, but once they had settled in the coastal plains, they tended to merge with the locals and adapt themselves to the relative ease of urban life.

Later the former conquerors, who formed the local aristocracy, readily became a spoil to their mountain kinsmen. Eventually, this state of affairs would allow the Romans to exploit the worsening situation and support the Campanians against the Samnites, an action that was to set in train the Samnite wars (343–341 BC, 327–304 BC, 298–290 BC). Even by themselves the Samnites were sufficiently warlike and numerous to cause concern, and their mutual hostility with Rome was deep rooted. In 82 BC the Samnites, just six years after the termination of the Social War, in which they had played a leading role, for the last time in history strapped on their armour and marched down from their Apennine fastness. Realizing that Rome lay at their mercy, they dashed towards the capital 'to pull down and destroy the tyrant city' (Velleius Paterculus *Historiae Romanae* 2.72.2).

OPPOSING COMMANDERS

SPARTACUS THE THRACIAN

There is no doubt at all over Spartacus' skill as a military commander, and to his natural flair he soon added valuable experience. But of the man himself, his personality, faults and foibles, we know nothing, for as we peer across the dividing centuries we only see the stylized, shadowy spectre of a rebel and a hero. Plenty is known about his achievements, however, mainly because in his *Life of Crassus* Plutarch illumined Spartacus' nobility of character – a quality Plutarch felt that Crassus, whom he clearly disliked, signally lacked. So Spartacus is described at some length in order to show what a wretched fellow Crassus was.

Roman sources provide no names for gladiators for at least the first hundred years of *munera*. Then, in the last third of the 2nd century BC, the satirist Lucilius, the great uncle of Pompey who had fought at the siege of Numantia, mentions a famous victor and a despised loser by name:

> In the public show given by the Flacci was a certain Aeserninus, a Samnite, a nasty fellow, worthy of that life and station. He was matched with Pacideianus, who was by far the best of all the gladiators since the creation of man. (Lucilius fr. 150 Marx)

By the way, the development of stage names, many of them erotic or heroic, came much later when gladiators were becoming stars by fighting and surviving several fights. Even so, with the exception of Spartacus, none really earned a significant place in recorded history.

His name may indicate that Spartacus was a descendant of the dynasty of the Spartokids, founded by Spartokos (or Spartakos) I, the Thracian ruler of the Cimmerian Bosporus in the late 5th century BC (Diodoros 12.31.1, 36.1, 16.93.1), while a Thracian 'Sparadokos', father of Seuthes of the Odrysae, is also known (Thucydides 2.101.5). But who was the gladiator named Spartacus?

Little is known about this remarkable character beyond the events of the rebellion, and the surviving ancient accounts are often contradictory. According to one, Spartacus had spent some years serving as a paid auxiliary for the Romans and then, having turned against them, became a 'deserter, then a bandit, and finally, thanks to his bodily strength, a gladiator' (Florus *Epitome* 3.20.8). The Romans, as we would naturally expect, were fond of declaring that their most dangerous opponents were always those they had trained themselves, and even no lesser an authority than Caesar himself says

that the Spartacan army was created 'to some extent by the military training and discipline that they had acquired from their Roman masters' (*Bellum Gallicum* 1.40.6). Whatever the truth of the matter, he had certainly gained some experience of military command before being captured and sent to the school of gladiators at Capua.

Varro, a learned antiquarian scholar who served as a legate with Pompey both in the Sertorian War (82–72 BC) and in the east, on sea and land, wrote on just about everything imaginable, including of course on rural science. In one lost work by him, there was an intriguing reference to Spartacus: 'Although he was an innocent man, Spartacus was condemned to a gladiatorial school' (quoted in Flavius Sosipater Charisius *Ars Grammatica* 1.133 Keil). Spartacus was certainly a freeborn Thracian, as corroborated by Plutarch (*Crassus* 8.2) and Appian (*Bellum civilia* 1.116), whereas Athenaios' statement that he was 'a slave, a Thracian by origin' (6.272f) refers only to his status at the time of his escape. Here it is important to note that the neat change from '*nomadikou*' to '*maidikou*' in Plutarch *Crassus* 8.2 is due to Konrad Ziegler (1955: 248–50); the transmitted text is corrupted and instead of 'a Thracian of nomadic stock', the name of the Thracian tribe of the Maedi is very likely here. Ziegler argues that Spartacus was a prisoner of war from the Maedi of the central Strymon Valley (south-western Bulgaria), acquired in Rome's campaigns of either 85 BC or 76 BC (e.g. Diodoros 39.8.1, Appian *Mithridatica* 55).

Free Thracian tribes probably supplied auxiliaries for the Roman forces in Macedonia, whose governors mounted a number of punitive campaigns against local tribes in the seventies BC. Then, to counter the growing threat of the Pontic king, Mithridates VI, to Bithynia on the eastern border of Thrace,

Spartacus' movements, summer 73 BC

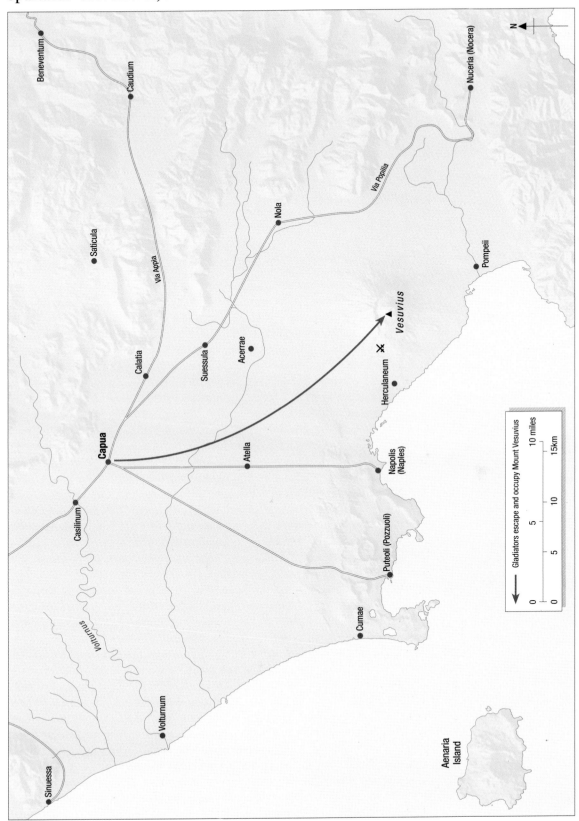

the Romans began to push into Thrace. That could have driven Spartacus to desert the Romans and fight against them in an attempt to stop the expansion of Rome's power into his tribal homeland. It is quite possible.

Of course it is not certain that the rebel slaves were a homogeneous group under the sole leadership of Spartacus, and it is difficult to believe this was indeed the case. While this is the unspoken assumption of the ancient sources, we do hear of other leaders – Crixus, Oenomaus, Castus and Gannicus. Plutarch does not introduce Spartacus until the occupation of Mount Vesuvius, where the gladiators chose three leaders, Spartacus being one of them, and indeed being considered the first amongst equals (*prôtos* in Plutarch's Greek, cf. Sallust *Historiae* 3.90, *princeps gladiatorum*); the other two being Crixus and Oenomaus, who were Gauls according to Orosius (5.24.1). Florus (*Epitome* 3.20.3) has them escaping with Spartacus from the gladiatorial training school, whereas Appian (*Bellum civilia* 1.116), while agreeing that they were gladiators, shows them emerging as Spartacus' subordinates once raiding and pillaging from Vesuvius was in progress. On the other hand, Livy (*Periochae* 95) suggests Crixus and Spartacus were co-leaders (Oenomaus not being mentioned here), while Orosius (5.24.1) suggests that all three were more or less equal leaders when Vesuvius was occupied.

Yet it seems that it was Spartacus who supplied the spark, the brains, and we should marvel at the leadership skills exhibited by him. He was a mere gladiator, with no organized government behind him, no trained soldiers at his beck and call, no arsenal of weapons and equipment upon which he could draw. Beginning with nothing, Spartacus organized, equipped, trained and fed an army, a difficult and brilliant stroke of policy. The rebellion certainly gave him the perfect opportunity to assert a natural capacity for leadership. We should note a comparison with a Roman commander, who held his position by reason of his rank rather than his fighting qualities, and invariably depended on the fighting qualities of the Roman legion instead of knowledge of strategy and tactics.

Appian, who generally paints a rather more damning picture of Spartacus than Plutarch, does however give us two very interesting pieces of information about him. First, Spartacus divided equally the spoils won from victories or raids, and this general rule of equal treatment for everybody attracted more followers to his camp. Second, Spartacus banned merchants from bringing in gold or silver and did not allow anyone in his camp to possess any. So there was no trade in these precious metals. Then again he did encourage the trade in iron and copper, and as a result of this common-sense policy the slaves 'had plenty of raw material and were well equipped and made frequent raiding expeditions' (Appian *Bellum civilia* 1.117).

MARCUS LICINIUS CRASSUS

When he was assigned the task of putting down the Spartacan rebellion, Marcus Licinius Crassus was no stranger to military command. Like Pompey, the young Crassus had joined Lucius Cornelius Sulla during his second march on Rome. Unlike Pompey, however, Crassus had a personal feud with the Marian faction. His father had led the opposition to Marius during his bloodstained seventh consulship, and had anticipated his fate by stabbing himself to death (Cicero *De oratore* 3.10). In the resulting purge Crassus' elder brother was liquidated and the family's estates seized. Yet at the time of the rebellion Crassus, who was now in his early forties, was one of the wealthiest men in Rome and allegedly the city's greatest landlord.

Crassus had laid the foundations of his monstrous wealth in the time of terror under Sulla, buying up confiscated property of the proscribed at rock-bottom prices. He had multiplied it by acquiring depreciated or burnt-out houses for next to nothing and rebuilding them with his workforce of hundreds of specially trained slaves (Plutarch *Crassus* 2.3–4). Yet for Crassus money was not the means to profit and pleasure, however, but the means to power. And though, like any shrewd businessman, he did his utmost to increase his personal fortune by all kinds of investments and shady deals, his primary concern was to extend his political influence. A genial host, a generous dispenser of loans and a shrewd patron of the potentially useful, he ensured his money bought him immense influence. Half the Senate was in his debt, and a debt taken out with Crassus always came with heavy political interest.

No one, Crassus is reported to have boasted, could call himself rich until he was able to support a legion on his yearly income (Pliny *Historia Naturalis* 33.134). The cost of this is easily determinable. In 52 BC Crassus' rival of old, Pompey, would receive from the state 1,000 talents out of which he was expected to feed and maintain his soldiers (Plutarch *Pompey* 55.7). At the time Pompey's provinces were Iberia and Africa, in which there were stationed six legions (ibid. 52.3 with Appian *Bellum civilia* 2.24). One talent was worth 6,000 Greek *drachmae*, which was equivalent to 6,000 Roman *denarii* or 24,000 *sestertii*. Thus six legions cost six million *denarii* to

Grave marker (Aphrodisias, inv. 1067) of a gladiator, a Thracian or *thrēx*. It was not until the Principate that the trademark equipment of a *thrēx* would consist of a wide-brimmed crested helmet with visor (*galea*), quilted fabric leg and arm defences (*fasciae et manicae*), high greaves (*ocrea*) on both legs, a small, round or square shield (*parma*), and a short, slightly-curved sword (*sica*). (Fields-Carré Collection)

Grave marker (Aphrodisias, inv. 1070) of the gladiator Phortis, a *retiarius*. Another speciality of the Principate, a 'net-man' was equipped with a quilted fabric arm protector (*manica*), which was often topped with a bronze shoulder-piece (*galerus*), fish net (*rete*), three-pronged fish fork (*fascina*), and a small dagger (*pugio*). The *retiarius* was the only type of gladiator whose head and face was uncovered. (Fields-Carré Collection)

maintain, the cost for one would be four million *sestertii* per annum. But here we should remember that this is Crassus' minimum qualification for the epithet rich; Pliny, in the aforementioned passage, says Crassus' fortune was worth 200 million *sestertii*. Obviously Crassus was one who could support not only a legion but a whole army.

Fleeing the bounty hunters, the young Crassus had left Marian Rome and made it to Iberia where his father's spell as proconsul had been immensely profitable. Despite being a fugitive, he had taken the unheard-of step of recruiting his own private army, a force of some 2,500 clients and dependants. Crassus had then led it around the Mediterranean, sampling alliances with other anti-Marian factions, before finally sailing for Greece and throwing his lot in with Sulla. At the battle of Porta Collina (2 November 82 BC) he would shatter the Samnite left wing and thereby save Sulla. Sadly, his besetting sin of avarice lost him the favour of the dictator soon afterwards when he added to the proscription lists the name of a man whose property he wanted. Sulla discovered this, and never trusted Crassus again (Plutarch *Crassus* 6.6-7).

Fabulously wealthy he was, but his driving ambition was military glory. He took on the command against Spartacus when many other senators were reluctant to do so. Because of the total humiliation that would have followed from it, an annihilating defeat at the hands of a slave army would have sunk any political career. Besides, as well as the unspeakable shame in such a defeat, there was little virtue in putting down slaves. Behind the acceptance of course lay Crassus' political rivalry with the supreme egotist, Pompey.

Crassus' first action on taking command was to revive an ancient and terrible form of punishment to strike mortal terror in his soldiers' hearts. He inflicted the fate of decimation on the reluctant members of two legions who had survived a recent hammering by Spartacus. He selected 500 soldiers who had run from the battle, then divided them in to 50 groups of ten. Each group of ten had to select a victim by lot from among them. Then the remaining nine were ordered to club the tenth man to death, the courageous along with the cowardly, while the rest of the army looked on (Plutarch *Crassus* 10.2-3, Appian *Bellum civilia* 1.118). Military discipline was re-imposed. At the same time, a warning was sent to the opposition that they could expect no mercy from a commander prepared to impose such sanctions upon his own men.

On fleeing the battlefield, many of the legionaries had left their weapons to increase the rebels' already growing store. Apparently Crassus issued new arms on payment of a deposit. In later life Crassus would be indicted with seducing a Vestal Virgin, but procedures had brought to light that the nocturnal visits to the small temple of Vesta had been nothing but business affairs and not of the heart. Apparently the lady in question, Licinia was her name, owned a desirable residence in the suburbs and Crassus wanted to buy it at a very favourable price, hence the amorous attention and the subsequent scandal. 'It was his avarice that cleared him of having corrupted the lady', Plutarch explains, 'but he did not did not let Licinia alone until he had acquired the property' (*Crassus* 1.2). Such a farce as this must have rocked all Rome.

Crassus' avarice is, indeed, emphasized from the very start of Plutarch's biography. Even among his mature contemporaries Crassus' wealth was proverbial, as was his willingness to acquire it by any means whatsoever. Wealth was to be obtained by inheritance and expanded by agriculture and by the spoils of war. There were other forms of making money such as mining, usury, tax farming, and trade, but these had to be left to the *equites*, prosperous Romans below the senatorial order who did not compete for public office or hold provincial commands. Senators were held to a higher standard. Not so Crassus: he accumulated wealth by aggressively profiting from the misfortune of others. 'Certainly the Romans say', as Plutarch puts it, 'that in the case of Crassus many virtues were obscured by one vice, namely avarice' (*Crassus* 2.1). Indeed a similar point is made by the Roman historian Velleius Paterculus: 'Although Crassus was, in his general character, entirely upright and free from base desires, in his lust for money and his ambition for glory he knew no limits, and accepted no bounds' (*Historiae Romanae* 2.46.2).

Certainly his grisly and pointless end, which Plutarch elaborates with a dramatic description of the delivery of Crassus' freshly severed head to the Parthian king, was the result of an excess of ambition. It was tossed from hand to hand like a ball during the course of a performance of Euripides' *Bacchae*, which the king, who 'knew Greek and was well versed in Greek literature' (*Crassus* 33.2), had presented on the afternoon of the victory over Rome. The Spartacan rebellion and the Parthian campaign were the two most important military undertakings of Crassus' career, and Plutarch's view of the dangers of naked ambition is made the more tellingly when the reader understands that the success of the first led directly to the catastrophe of the second in Crassus' desperate struggle to keep pace with Pompey (and Caesar), as his lust for glory led him towards Carrhae (Harran, Turkey), a caravan town shimmering in the arid wastes of northern Mesopotamia.

Marble bust (Copenhagen, Ny Carlsberg Glyptotek, inv. 749) found in the Tomb of the Licinii, Rome. It is possible that this represents the future triumvir Marcus Licinius Crassus. Unlike his predecessors, Crassus did not make the mistake of underestimating Spartacus. He saw the war as a way of furthering his political ambitions and satisfying his hunger for military glory. (Ny Carlsberg Glyptotek)

OPPOSING ARMIES

According to our sources, over a period of some two years the slave army won at least nine encounters and sacked at least four major towns. Indeed, many of the first-generation slaves, like Spartacus, may have previously seen military service in the armies of Rome or of the Hellenistic kings, or fought as tribal warriors in miscellaneous tribal wars.

As for the Romans, they attached a great deal of importance to training, and it is this that largely explains the formidable success of their army. 'And what can I say about the training of legions?' is the rhetorical question aired by Cicero. 'Put an equally brave, but untrained soldier in the front line and he will look like a woman' (*Tusculanae disputationes* 2.16.37). The basic aim of this training was to give the legions superiority over the 'barbarian' in battle. Therefore Roman strength lay in the set-piece battle, the decisive clash of opposing armies that settled the issue one way or another. In this role the legion usually performed very well. Still, Spartacus was no 'barbarian' general, nor was his army a 'barbarian' horde.

THE SLAVE ARMY

The evidence in the sources constantly reminds us that the varied ethnic and cultural backgrounds of Spartacus' host make its spirit inherently unstable. Yet this heterogeneous body of men just released from slavery became a surprisingly effective fighting force that repeatedly demonstrated that its members could stand up to the disciplined legions of Rome. Spartacus never had cavalry, such as Hannibal did, but he did put such a unit together, according to Florus, 'by breaking in wild horses that they encountered' (*Epitome* 3.20.7). Even so, being an infantry-based force, the age-old military virtues of determination, endurance, ingenuity, boldness, and courage enabled Spartacus to keep his slave army from being destroyed and to prevent his infant rebellion from being crushed.

Naturally it can be argued that in such a vast multiracial gathering, communications among its members would have been difficult to say the least. However, it would be naive to assume such an argument as it glosses over the necessary presumption that if foreign slaves and their Roman masters had to establish basic forms of communication in order for work to be accomplished, then such a system of communication could be exploited by slaves for their own purposes. Moreover, the development of pidgin and creole languages in modern slave societies shows that language barriers between slaves were problems that could be surmounted, and the same can be imagined for the army of Spartacus where the *lingua franca* was probably a debased form of Latin.

Spartacus' followers, it is reported, were mainly Gauls, Germans, or other Thracians (Sallust *Historiae* 3.96, Plutarch *Crassus* 8.1, 9.5, 6, Livy *Periochae* 97). It has been suggested that the Gauls and the Germans, along with the Thracians, were all from the Balkans, recently brought to Italy as the human spoils of war. However, we must not forget the trade in providing slaves to Italy from Gaul itself. This human commerce was brought along major slave-trading networks – from northern Europe, from lands north and east of the Rhine, and from the lands of the upper reaches of the Danube – to the western Mediterranean down the Rhône to Arelate (Arles), Massilia (Marseille) and other seaports in Gallia Transalpina. Obviously these slaves were mainly Gauls and Germans, but other slaves came from the region north of the lower Danube and the Black Sea. The main slave-trading route here ran through Thrace to seaports on the northern shores of the Aegean. The fact that Thrace was a crossroads in this traffic in humans, and itself fed significant numbers of its population into the Mediterranean basin as slaves, is particularly significant in understanding the number of Thracians found among the followers of Spartacus.

'Ludovisi Gaul' (Rome, MNR Palazzo Altemps, inv. 8608), Roman copy of a bronze originally dedicated to Athena Bringer of Victory by Attalos I of Pergamon (r. 241–197 BC). This statue group is usually interpreted as a Gallic chieftain and his wife, bravely pre-empting capture by suicide. It rightly reminds us that women were an integral and important part of the slave army. (Fields-Carré Collection)

Like the two earlier slave wars most of the slaves who joined the Spartacan rebellion, whatever their provenance, were simple agricultural labourers and herdsmen. Agricultural slaves, namely those who cultivated cereals, vines, olives and other arboreal crops, worked under close supervision. According to the handbooks on agriculture, as already noted, the ideal was to have the slaves deployed in work gangs of 13 to 16 people. For purposes of surveillance and security, during the night or at times they were not labouring in the fields, the slaves were shackled and penned in quarters known as *ergastula*, or 'work barracks'. Worked like animals, the slaves were housed like animals.

The open expanses of southern Italy and Sicily were more arid and could not easily sustain a viable market-orientated agriculture based on cash crops. In these regions, therefore, slave owners developed a different kind of agriculture that mixed the cultivation of cereals with the raising of large herds of cattle and sheep, sometimes pigs and goats. Men like the Roman *eques* Publius Aufidius Pontianus, a wealthy landowner of Amiternum in the heart of the Sabine highlands, who brought, as Spartacus' Roman contemporary Varro tells us, herds 'in furthest Umbria' to have them driven 'to the pastures of Metapontum and to market at Heraclea' (*On Agriculture* 2.9.6), a distance of some 450km. Under the care of slave herdsmen, *pastores*, such herds spent the summer in the mountains and the winter on the plains. Obviously these slaves could not be constrained by chains or housed in *ergastula* each night. They had to be free to follow the herds. In addition, they had to be armed to protect the animals from predators, four-legged and two-legged variety alike.

Spartacus' & Crixus' movements, spring 72 BC

Spartacus and his followers trek northward to the Po valley

Having split from Spartacus, Crixus and his followers are cornered and destroyed near Mount Garganus

In Sicily, in the decades preceding the First Slave War, Roman and Italian landowners consciously established their slave herdsmen in the practice of banditry as a form of economic self-help. Freelance raiding and pillaging, encouraged by the landowner, allowed him to escape the onerous burdens connected with the surveillance and maintenance of distantly roaming bands of his slave herdsmen at the expense of unprotected village and farm dwellers who became the target of widespread acts of banditry. Consequently Sicily was reduced to an island infested with bands of slave herdsmen who roamed at will throughout the land 'like detachments of soldiers' (Diodoros 35.2.1). Despite formal complaints, Roman governors hesitated to enforce the rule of law and to repress brigandage because of the pressure brought to bear on them by the powerful landowners.

In 71 BC, the year the Spartacan rebellion was extinguished, Cicero delivered a forensic speech, the *Pro Tullio*, which survives only in fragments. But its interest for us is considerable, for Cicero 'takes us into the wild hill-country of Lucania' where 'we find cattle-barons and their hired hands, armed slaves that is, raiding and plundering each other's herds and homesteads' (Stockton 1971: 19). Cicero's client, Marcus Tullius, had in fact had his villa in the region of Thurii razed to the ground and his slaves butchered by an armed band belonging to a certain Publius Fabius, though Tullius' own *pastores* were quite capable of similar atrocities.

'Dying Gaul' (Rome, Musei Capitolini, inv. 747), Roman copy of a bronze originally dedicated to Athena Bringer of Victory by Attalos I of Pergamon (r. 241–197 BC). The oversize warrior was glamorized soon after its discovery as a 'Dying Gladiator' – 'butchered to make a Roman holiday', as Byron puts it in *Childe Harold*. Yet the torque, moustache and spiky hair are very much Gaulish traits. (Fields-Carré Collection)

The central natural advantage of slave herdsmen was their freedom of movement and the possession of arms. From Varro's remarks on *pastores* in the agricultural handbook he published in 37 BC, near the end of his long and active life, a sense of what they were like can be gleaned. Preferably, Varro says, herdsmen who pastured livestock for sustained periods without returning daily to the farmstead were to be physically mature, boys being of little use for this kind of graft, and well above average in fitness, in view of the rigours of their work and the terrain to which they were daily exposed. 'You should choose men', he explains, 'of powerful physique, fast-moving and nimble, who are not clumsy when they move their limbs, and are just not able to follow after the flock but also to defend it from predatory beasts or brigands, who can lift loads up onto the backs of the pack animals, are good at sprinting and at hitting their target' (*On Agriculture* 2.10.3). Obviously a familiarity with weapons was standard for these men.

The indefatigable Varro, who owned land at both ends of the Samnium-Apulia transhumance route and possessed large stocks of cattle and sheep, observes further that Iberians were not at all suitable for herding but that Gauls were, a remark implying that even in his day herdsmen were often new slaves (*On Agriculture* 2.10.4). So habitually armed and enjoying a considerable freedom of movement though answerable to a *magister pecoris* or 'herd master', as they moved their charges along the drove-trails between mountain and plain, such men, new to slavery, used to a certain independence and to relying on their own wits and resources for survival, might well join Spartacus willingly.

Reconstruction of a metal smelting furnace or hearth, archaeological open day Bobigny, Seine-Saint-Denis. Charcoal was the preferred fuel for smelting (reduction of ore to metal), as it burned more slowly and evenly than wood, and since artificial draught (fan or bellows) was used the temperature would be controlled more easily. The blacksmiths in Spartacus' camp would have employed the same smelting techniques. (Fields-Carré Collection)

The *magister pecoris* Varro mentions was to be a man physically strong but 'older than the rest and also more experienced' (*On Agriculture* 2.10.2). Such slaves, exercising managerial functions, were used to commanding authority and to being obeyed. Likewise the *vilicus* in arable farming, who organized the day-to-day finances of the farm, brought and sold materials, and supervised the annual cycle of work. He also set the work details and controlled the workforce (Cato *On Agriculture* 5.1–5). He was to be 'of middle age and of strong body and be knowledgeable in agricultural work' (Columella *On Agriculture* 1.8.3). The *vilicus* equated with *magister pecoris* and these elite slaves provided the managerial skills and technical know-how needed to run farms and homesteads exploited by slave labour. Since they already had experience in controlling and directing the work and behaviour of slaves, they could easily apply the same skills to leading the rebels of Spartacus' army.

The core of the slaves who incited and led the rebellion, however, were not *vilici* or *magistri pecoris*, but those who had been trained in bloodshed and soaked in violence, not as soldiers but as gladiators. These were men of the sword, hard, angry men, disciplined to inflict death on others, and, most likely, eventually be killed by a superior killer. It was with their help that Spartacus was able to transform what was essentially a ravaging band of amateur bandits, seeking a prime opportunity for raiding and looting, into a formidable fighting force.

Initially all the arms this fighting force had were taken in booty, purchased or forged, which was sufficient only for part of the slave army. The rest were armed with sickles, pitchforks, rakes, flails, axes, hatchets and other implements of the field that could be called into service for battle purposes, or, where even these were lacking, flourished fire-hardened sticks, sharpened poles, hobnailed clubs and other wooden points and bludgeons. These makeshift weapons were as much for defence as for damaging the enemy, but naturally nothing was to be scorned.

Sallust (*Historiae* 3.102-103) talks of men skilled in weaving and basket-making who were able to compensate for the lack of proper shields by making small circular bucklers. Frontinus (*Strategemata* 1.7.6) provides us with further details, saying these were constructed out of vine branches and then covered with the skins of animals. Florus (*Epitome* 3.20.6) has the same details concerning the 'rough shields', as he calls them, but adds that swords and spearheads were forged by melting down and reworking leg irons taken from *ergastula*. Sallust however, in a fragment referring to the campaign against Varinius, says the rebels needed 'to harden their spears in the fire, and give them (apart from the necessary warlike appearance) the capability of inflicting almost as much damage as steel' (*Historiae* 3.96). Exact details may differ, but the theme is the same, that is, initially the rebels had to equip themselves with makeshift weapons.

TOP
Selection of iron implements and weapons, archaeological open day Bobigny, Seine-Saint-Denis. Blacksmiths did not have the technology to melt iron for casting, so instead it was forged (heated and hammered) using techniques quite adequate for producing very effective implements and weapons. One source of iron for Spartacus' blacksmiths would have been the shackles and chains plundered from *ergastula*. (Fields Carré Collection)

BOTTOM
Reconstruction Gallic arms and armour, archaeological open day Bobigny, Seine-Saint-Denis. Here we see the characteristic long slashing-sword of the Gallic warrior, a weapon designed to either hack an opponent to pieces or to beat him to a bloody pulp. It is highly conceivable that such swords were forged by Spartacus' blacksmiths for use by the Gauls of his army. (Fields-Carré Collection)

The herdsmen who came to join Spartacus were, unsurprisingly, better armed and equipped. These men were strong and wirily built, accustomed to spending their days and nights in the open air, no matter how inclement the weather. Hunting spears, shepherd staffs, knotty cudgels and slings served them as weapons. Their attire consisted of the skins of wolves or the hides of wild boars. In addition they were accompanied by watchdogs, calf-sized brutes with extremely fierce tempers. Such wild, wind-burned men had nothing to lose and everything to gain through war, and, as Plutarch says, some of them, especially those with legs of iron, were exceedingly useful 'as scouts and light-armed troops' (*Crassus* 9.3).

According to Appian (*Bellum civilia* 1.116), Spartacus had weapons made for what had become, in his reckoning, a force of 70,000 after the defeat of Varinius, while at Thurii his followers 'brought lots of iron and bronze and did not do anything to harm people who traded in these metals. In this way they came to be well supplied with a lot of war material' (ibid. 1.117). Naturally

the most fruitful sources of ready-made arms and equipment were the Roman armies the rebels confronted and destroyed. So the capture of two Roman camps, those of Glaber and Cossinius, and their battlefield successes over Varinius produced more acquisitions.

Finally, we should speak of the role of women in the slave army. When Appian records that the rebels numbered some 70,000, he may have included the so-called non-combatants in his total. Before the rebellion began, many male slaves must have formed unions with female slaves, wives who were prepared in the event to follow their husbands in revolt. When Spartacus was sold as a slave he had with him a wife, also Thracian by origin, who remained with him after his transfer to Capua and participated in the revolt he led. Plutarch adds she was 'a prophetess and initiated into the ecstatic cult of Dionysos' (*Crassus* 8.3). Unfortunately no more is heard of her, and she is only mentioned by Plutarch because she interpreted the terrible significance of the snake that once coiled round his head without harming him while he slept. Plutarch gives her no name.

Which brings us to another of Plutarch's curious tales. The Romans were stealthily approaching the camp of a group of rebels led by Gannicus and Castus when they were spotted by a couple of women. These two had left the camp and gone up the nearby mountain to make, in Plutarch's words, 'ritual sacrifices' (*Crassus* 11.3). Sallust records the same incident, but states that the two women, Gauls, 'climbed up the mountain to spend their menstrual periods there' (*Historiae* 4.40). Either Plutarch misread the original Latin, or deliberately bowdlerized the text. Whatever, these two women were probably the wives of two of the rebels.

THE ROMAN ARMY

Caius Marius has often been credited with taking the decisive steps that laid the basis for the professional standing army of the Principate. Rome was now the dominant power in the Mediterranean basin and the annual levying of what was in effect a part-time citizen militia was incompatible with the running and maintenance of a world empire. Moreover, decades of war overseas had turned out thousands of trained soldiers, and many of them would have found themselves strangers to civilian life after their years of service abroad. The army had been their life and Marius called them back home. But besides these leathery old veterans of Rome's diverse campaigns, Marius also enrolled another more numerous kind of volunteer: the men with nothing.

A census of all adult male citizens recorded the value of their property and divided them accordingly into five property classes. However, those citizens who could not declare to the censors the minimum census qualification for enrolment in Class V were excluded from military service. Lacking the means to provide themselves arms, these poor citizens were listed in the census simply as the *capite censi* or 'head count'. However, Marius was not content to supplement his army by only drawing upon 'the bravest soldiers from the Latin towns' (Sallust *Bellum Iugurthinum* 84.2). Thus, of all the reforms attributed to Marius, the opening of the ranks to *capite censi* in 107 BC has obviously attracted the unanimous disapproval of ancient writers, a sentiment best put by his near-contemporary Sallust:

> Some said he did this because he could not get enough of a better kind; others, that he wanted to curry favour with men of low condition, since he owed to them his fame and advancement. And indeed, if a man is ambitious for power, he can have no better supporters than the poor: they are not concerned about their own possessions, since they have none, and whatever will put something in their pockets is right and proper in their eyes. (Sallust *Bellum Iugurthinum* 86.2)

And so Marius stands accused of paving the way for the so-called lawless, greedy soldiery whose activities were thought to have contributed largely to the decline and fall of the Republic a few generations later.

Yet we should not lose sight of the fact that Marius was not the first to enrol the *capite censi*. Rome was ruled by an aristocratic oligarchy embedded in the Senate, which disarmed the weary and cheated poor by pressing swords in their hands, the assumption being that anyone who became a soldier became thereby once and for all one of the props of the ruling order. Thus at times of extreme crisis in the past the Senate had impressed them, along with convicts and slaves, for service as legionaries. In the dark days following the crushing

A Roman praetor or consul was preceded by lictors, each carrying on his left shoulder a ceremonial bundle of bound, wooden rods (*fasces*) with a single-headed axe (*securis*) embedded in them. These symbolized, six for a praetor and 12 for a consul, the power of the magistrate to discipline by the use of physical force. This slab is built into a fountain at Paestum. (Fields-Carré Collection)

defeat at Cannae (216 BC), for instance, two legions were enlisted from slave-volunteers (Livy 22.57.11, 23.32.1). Marius was merely carrying one stage further a process visible during the 2nd century BC, by which the prescribed property qualification for service in the army was eroded and became less meaningful. Now the only real prerequisites were that of Roman citizenship and a willingness to go soldiering.

Noticeably the ancient sources do not say that Marius swept away the qualification, or changed the law on eligibility. On the contrary, he merely appealed to the *capite censi* for volunteers, whom he could equip from state funds under the legislation drawn up by Caius Gracchus in 123 BC, by which the state was responsible for equipping the soldier fighting in its defence (Plutarch *Caius Gracchus* 5.1). Even before Gracchus' *lex militaria*, there had been a progressive debasement of the property threshold for Class V from 11,000 *asses* to 4,000 *asses* (Livy 1.43.8, cf. Polybios 6.19.2). In 123 BC, as one of the tribunes of the people, Gracchus himself reduces the property qualification again, setting the minimum at 1,500 *asses* (Gabba 1976: 7–10). This last represents a very small amount of property indeed, almost certainly insufficient to maintain an average-sized family, but the effect was an ongoing attempt to increase the number of citizens that qualified for military service.

Marius' reform should be seen as the logical conclusion to this development, something Rome's overseas ventures on increasingly far-flung fields had exacerbated. What he did was to legalize a process that had been present for about a century and that the Senate had failed to implement, that is, opening up the army to all citizens regardless of their property, arming them at state expense, and recruiting them not through the *dilectus*, the annual levy, but on a volunteer basis. With Marius the traditional link between property and defence of the state was broken forever. What is more, by the enfranchizing laws of 90–89 BC the recruiting area for those who could serve in the legions was extended to all of Italy south of the Po. So the *socii* – Latin and Italian allies – disappeared, and the Roman army was now composed of legions of citizen-soldiers recruited throughout peninsular Italy, and contingents of non-Italians serving either as volunteers or as mercenaries.

Marius is also credited with changes in tactical organization, namely he abolished the maniple (*manipulus*, pl. *manipuli*) and substituted the cohort as the standard tactical unit of the legion. The manipular legion of the middle Republic had been split into distinct battle lines. Behind a screen of *velites*, or light-armed troops, the first line comprised the *hastati* ('spearmen'), the second line, the soldiers in their prime, composed of the *principes* ('chief men'), while the oldest and more mature men were assigned to the third line and called the *triarii* ('third-rank men'). There were 10 maniples and 20 centuries in each battle line, making a total of 30 maniples and 60 centuries to the manipular legion. While Marius maintained the centuries and the maniples for administrative purposes, he chose to divide his legion into 10 cohorts, each of which consisted of three maniples, one drawn from each of the three lines of *hastati*, *principes* and *triarii*.

The cohort (*cohors*, pl. *cohortes*) as a formation of three maniples was not an entirely novel innovation, as it appears to have been in use as a tactical, as opposed to an administrative, expedient from the time of the Second Punic War. Polybios, in his account (11.23.1, cf. 33) of the battle of Ilipa (206 BC), pauses to explain the meaning of the term *cohors* to his Greek readership. Surprisingly, it receives no mention in his detailed account of army organization neither in the sixth book nor in his comparison of legion and phalanx in the eighteenth book, although, it should be stated, there is little on tactics in both these narratives. On the other hand, some have detected, in Sallust's account (*Bellum Iugurthinum* 49.6) of the operations of Quintus Caecilius Metellus (*cos.* 109 BC) against Iugurtha (109–108 BC), the last reference to maniples manoeuvring as the sole tactical unit of the battle line Hence a belief that Marius swept them away either in 106 BC or during his preparations in 104 BC for the war with the Cimbri and Teutones.

It is recognized that the battle of Pydna (168 BC) was the triumph of the Roman maniple over the Macedonian phalanx, and this disposition was adequate until Rome came to meet an opponent who adopted a method of attack different from the slow methodical advance of the phalanx with its 'bristling rampart of outstretched pikes' (Plutarch *Aemilius Paullus* 19.1). The tactics of the Germanic and Celtic tribes, the latter armed with a long, two-edged sword designed for slashing, was to stake everything upon a vigorous onslaught at the start of the battle, beating down the shields of the opposition and breaking into their formation. This was a terrifying thing, and at times could swiftly sweep away an opponent – especially a nervous one – but if it was halted the tribesmen would tend to lose their enthusiasm and retreat quickly. To meet this brutal method of attack, where the perpetrators believed that fighting power increased in proportion to the size of the mass, the formation in three fixed battle lines of maniples was unsuited. The units themselves were fairly small and shallow, and an attack strongly pressed home might easily overcome their resistance. In the war against the Celtic Insubres (225 BC) the *hastati* of the front line had attempted to circumvent this difficulty by substituting their *pila* for the thrusting-spears of the *triarii* stationed in the rear (Polybios 2.33.4).

Yet the small size of the maniple was a major weakness against such a style of fighting, and Marius decided to strengthen his front line of defence by increasing the size of the individual units. Thus the cohort took the place of the maniple as the tactical unit of the Marian legion, which was now organized into

10 cohorts, each of which was subdivided into six centuries. In effect the old threefold battle array was cut into 10 slices from front to back, with the cohort being a large but manageable unit of 480 men. When deployed for battle, the 10 cohorts of a legion still formed up in the traditional *triplex acies*, with four in the front line, then a line of three, and finally three more at the rear.

Another sound argument for placing a definite decision in favour of the cohort at the time of Marius could be that, with the lowering of the property qualification and its eventual abolition, the legionaries were now equipped by the state at public expense. Consequently, variations in equipment originally linked to differing financial statuses now ceased to have any *raison d'être*. All legionaries were now equipped with a bronze Montefortino helmet, a mail shirt (*lorica hamata*), the *scutum*, two *pila*, one heavy the other light, and *gladius Hispaniensis*, plus a dagger (*pugio*). Greaves disappeared, except on centurions.

The legionary, like all professional foot soldiers before his day and after, was grossly overloaded – alarmingly so, according to some accounts. Cicero wrote of 'the toil, the great toil, of the march: the load of more than half a month's provisions, the load of any and everything that might be required, the load of the stake for entrenchment' (*Tusculanae disputationes* 2.16.37). Normally, perhaps, a legionary carried rations for three days, not the two weeks to which Cicero refers. However, it has been estimated that the legionary was burdened with equipment weighing as much as 35kg if not more.

It appears, therefore, that another of Marius' apparent reforms was to reduce the size of the baggage train (*impedimenta*). The legionaries now had to shoulder much of their gear: bedroll and cloak, three or more days' ration of grain, a bronze cooking pot (*trulleus*) and mess tin (*patera*), a metal canteen or leather flask, a sickle for cutting grain and forage, a wicker basket for earth

moving, either a pickaxe (*dolabra*) or an iron-shod wooden spade (*pala*), a length of rope, and a stake (*pilum muralis*) for fortifying the overnight marching camp. This gear was slung from a T-shaped pole (*furca*), and Plutarch says (*Marius* 13.1) the soldiers were nicknamed *muli Mariani*, Marius' mules, a wry description that would remain in popular currency. On the march each mess-unit of eight legionaries, the *contubernium*, was also allowed one four-legged mule to carry the heavier items such as its leather tent and millstones.

The natural implication of Marius' decision to enrol poor citizens in the army was that the newly raised legions would not all automatically cease to exist when the men where dismissed from duty. In effect, the legion became a permanent organization into which new recruits could be added, keeping the same name and number throughout its existence. To mark this change in status, Marius gave each legion a permanent standard to represent it. The republican legion, according to the elder Pliny (*Historia Naturalis* 10.5.16.), originally had five standards: eagle, wolf, minotaur, horse, and boar. He places the adoption of the silver eagle (*aquila*) as the supreme standard of all legions precisely in 104 BC, at the start of preparations for the war against the northern tribes. This selection of the eagle, a bird of prey associated with Iuppiter, is thus firmly credited to Marius.

The new standard was carried into battle by a senior standard-bearer, the *aquilifer*, second only to a centurion in rank. It was under the personal care of the *primus pilus* ('first spear'), the chief centurion of the legion who nominally commanded the first century in the first cohort. While its safe custody was equivalent to the continuance of the legion as a fighting unit, however depleted in numbers, its loss brought the greatest ignominy on any survivors and could result in the disbandment of the legion in disgrace. Frontinus, for instance, reports that after the defeat of the rebels led by Castus and Gannicus, Crassus was able to recover 'five *aquilae* and twenty-six *signa*' (*Strategemata* 2.5.34).

The *aquila* not only worked to increase the loyalty and devotion of soldiers to the legion through fostering a corporate identity, but it was also reflective of the sweeping away of the old class divisions within the Roman army. And so legionaries who viewed the army as a career, not simply as an interruption to normal life, came to identify very strongly with their legion, and these units developed, in the fullness of time, tremendous corporate spirit. Admittedly an old provisional legion could be a first-class fighting unit, especially if seasoned by long service, but a new professional legion was on average better trained and disciplined than its predecessors, simply because it was more permanent. At the time of Marius, the legions were probably still reconstructed every year, but by Caesar's day they certainly began to retain their identity.

To sum up: in the ranks of Crassus' legions, that is, those legions that eventually extinguished the Spartacan rebellion, there were men of modest means, city-dwelling *proletarii* and their country cousins, the rural poor, whose dire poverty or meagre fields, indeed if they had smallholdings, made them willing recruits. There were individuals who had chosen the army as their profession, and their military world was firmly rooted in the *esprit de corps* of their legions. Many of them had taken their military oath with the hope of a land settlement at the end of their term of service and the promise of loot during it. Regardless of their social condition, these men were Roman and free, and thus saw themselves as far superior to any alien slave. Besides, even in a fight against slaves there would still be fruits of war.

OPPOSING PLANS

THE SPARTACAN PLAN

We have seen that Spartacus, through the force of his charismatic personality and military genius, was able to weld an amorphous, inarticulate, semi-barbarian host of 'slaves, deserters, and riffraff' (Appian *Bellum civilia* 1.117) into a formidable fighting force that managed to defeat nine Roman armies ranging from a few thousand untried recruits and time-served veterans, to tens of thousands of veteran legionaries.

There is absolutely no evidence that Spartacus ever held the bright vision of a new world and dreamed of abolishing slavery. There is a sad reality; the ancient world embraced slavery as part of the natural order of things. While his followers may have aimed at the extermination of their oppressors, they certainly wanted to free themselves and return to their tribal homelands, preferably after a spree of heavy looting in Italy. Sallust, a contemporary of Spartacus, does imply that he was one of the few 'prudent people' with 'free and noble minds' (*Historiae* 3.98) in the slave army and portrays him as trying repeatedly, if vainly, to restrain the baser instincts of the majority of his men who were bent on rape, murder, theft, and arson. Of course violence

Capua long remained a centre for gladiatorial combat and this Campanian city (along with Puteoli) possessed the largest permanent amphitheatre known (until overtaken by the Colosseum at Rome). It probably had an older one, which was subsequently superseded by the much larger facility we see here. It has been argued (Welch 1994) this amphitheatre was made specifically for the Caesarian veterans settled there by Octavianus. (Fototeca ENIT)

and unrest spread through the Italian countryside like some contagious disease, and we have to imagine that lawless elements everywhere took advantage of the state of rebellion.

Other sources, however, do present a more brutal side to Spartacus. Florus (*Epitome* 3.20.9) and Orosius (5.24.3) explicitly assert that Spartacus used Roman prisoners as gladiators in funeral games. Appian (*Bellum civilia* 1.117) is probably referring to one of these when he says Spartacus sacrificed 300 Roman soldiers on behalf of his dead friend Crixus. Appian also says (ibid. 1.119) that Spartacus crucified a Roman prisoner to inspire his followers by visually reminding them of the gruesome fate that awaited them if they did not win. He who commits brutalities frequently acts under the impulse of fear or apprehension that he himself will suffer the same fate.

As well as his character, the ancient authors also seem to be at odds about what the motives of Spartacus were. Appian (ibid. 1.117) and Florus (*Epitome* 3.20.11) write that he intended to march on Rome itself – although this may have been a reflection of Roman fears at the time. If Spartacus did intend to march on Rome, it was a goal subsequently abandoned. Plutarch (*Crassus* 9.5–6) only mentions that Spartacus wanted to escape northwards to Gallia Cisalpina and disperse his followers back to their homelands, wherever they might be. Nevertheless, this plan was also abandoned and the slave army turned back south again.

As mentioned before, it is difficult to believe that the rebel slaves were a homogeneous group under the sole leadership of Spartacus. Thus the question arises: was there genuine dissent arising from divergent aspirations? Perhaps they had been in Italy so long that despite their suffering they could not face the prospect of actually leaving. Moreover, they might have thought an attempt on Rome itself was possible, or at any rate continue on their career of looting the peninsula. Suppositions these may be, but it is a good guess that Spartacus saw the difficulties involved, for a successful crossing of the Alps would not necessarily guarantee freedom. Beyond lay more Roman territory and other Roman armies. Much better, so Spartacus probably reasoned, was to march south, cross to Sicily, where tens of thousands of slaves, full of memories of recent rebellions against Rome, could be raised in revolt.

It is Sallust who says that Caius Verres, when governor of Sicily, 'strengthened the fortifications on the shores closest to Italy' (*Historiae* 4.32). This was the same Verres immortalized by Cicero as an arch scoundrel, cut-throat and paragon of wickedness. When Verres was brought to trial on charges of extortion in 70 BC, Cicero, whom he prosecuted, purposefully maligned him by making his actions in Sicily seem even worse than those of the rebels

Relief (Munich, Glyptotek, inv. 364) showing a pair of gladiators, dated to 1st century BC. They are wearing thigh-length shirts of scale or iron mail – the shoulder 'doubling' suggests the latter – and Gallic-style helmets, and may represent Gallic nobles captured about the time of Caesar's conquest and subsequently condemned to fight in the arena. However, the sword (*gladius*, perhaps) and round shields are problematic. (Bibi Saint-Pol)

Spartacus' movements, summer 72 BC

Ancient Capua, now known as Santa Maria Capua Vetera, was destroyed by the Arabs in the 9th century and the survivors emigrated to Casilinum, on the south bank of the Volturnus (Volturno), taking their name with them. In Spartacus' day, however, Capua was 'queen among cities' (Florus *Epitome* 1.16.6), a metropolitan rival to Rome itself, a voluptuous city rightly famed for its gladiators and perfumes. (Fototeca ENIT)

of the Sicilian slave wars (e.g. *Verrines* 2.3.66, 4.112). Such debunking was to be Cicero's signature.

Verres – or so his prosecutor claimed – made over ten million *denarii* in embezzlement and swindles of all kinds in Sicily (e.g. ibid. 2.1.27). Even so, his governorship was in the years 73–71 BC, precisely when the Spartacan rebellion was raging on the mainland of southern Italy, directly opposite the island. Given the previous slave wars, there was a reasonable fear that the slaves of Sicily might rise again, and Verres seems to have taken the appropriately draconian measures (from the Roman point of view, of course) needed to keep his province under control. Interestingly, the very clever Cicero manages never to mention Spartacus by name in his vitriolic attack on Verres' administration.

It is Sallust too who says (*Historiae* 3.96, 98) a major bust-up between Spartacus and Crixus took place early on in the rebellion. With the praetor Varinius closing in, Spartacus sensibly wanted to escape north as soon as possible, but Crixus, with the Gauls and Germans behind him, imprudently wanted to fight the Romans head-on or at least had his heart set on plundering the peninsula.

Whatever the truth of the matter, the sources do indicate that Crixus and Oenomaus made a division of forces and split off with the Gauls and Germans to form a second slave army, that Oenomaus was soon killed, and that Crixus became the leader of the Gauls and Germans until he, too, died in battle and was, perhaps, succeeded by Castus and Gannicus (Orosius 5.24.6, Appian *Bellum civilia* 1.117, Plutarch *Crassus* 11.3, Frontinus *Strategemata* 2.5.34, Livy *Periochae* 96, 97). The quick of annihilation of Crixus and his people obviously placed Spartacus in a fatally weakened position. Spartacus and Crixus had shared the same goal, namely that age-old desire for freedom. Unfortunately for their cause they espoused conflicting strategies to reach it, that is to say, to escape Italy versus to stay in the peninsula to pillage and loot.

Spartacus and his followers refused to be Romans. They expressed no demand for Roman citizenship and its attendant rights. Rome, font of rationality, law, and order in the Occident, had nothing to offer them, so the prisoner of war wanted to return home, the debtor wanted his land back, the slave not born into slavery wanted his freedom back, while the slave born into slavery wanted to taste that freedom. We must, therefore, reject the dogma that Spartacus was a protagonist of the abolition of the institution of slavery or as a destroyer of Rome. There was no class struggle, nor any social revolution. The simple and sober truth was that he incarnated the determination of his followers never, never, never to be slaves again. Had he been merely an ambitious chief of brigands of small fighting capacity, it is most unlikely that he would have left Mount Vesuvius.

THE ROMAN PLAN

Warfare would not be warfare without an enemy, yet for Rome there were two types of warfare. One type of war, *bellum*, was the one recognized as genuine – a conflict between two legitimately established states, a battle between the armed forces of societies that shared manifest political structures and which fought according to recognized forms of combat. In this case the war was labelled 'real' or 'genuine', a *bellum iustum*. The other type of war was that waged by a state against inchoate, unstructured and socially inferior foes, in which case it was regarded as a 'bush' conflict or irregular war. A war of this type was usually qualified by some additional term that formally set it apart from a *bellum iustum* as, for instance, with the term 'slave', a *bellum servile* (e.g. Florus *Epitome* 3.19.2).

In the early stages of the rebellion the Senate, forgetting the lessons of recent history, looked upon the slaves as a motley crowd of desperadoes who would fly at the first sight of a Roman legion. How could such cowed and trembling slaves ever be and do anything else? And so any initial planning was very much influenced by the assumption that they were up against a few runaway slaves. It was not until the Senate handed Crassus the command against Spartacus that their so-called *bellum servile* became a full-blown *bellum iustum*.

Author Howard Fast once commented in an interview that aside from the gladiator fight between Kirk Douglas and Woody Strode nothing in Kubrick's epic film *Spartacus* could compare in dramatic intensity with the corresponding scenes in the novel. Yet the influence of the film has been tremendous – the scene 'I'm Spartacus!' is iconic – and for many today Spartacus is Douglas. (Wisconsin Center for Film and Theater Research)

THE CAMPAIGN

The Campanian metropolis of Capua, Italy's most voluptuous city and for over a century the main *entrepôt* for the training and housing of gladiators, was also the hotspot that produced the greatest gladiatorial sensation of all time. One day in the springtime of 73 BC, a group of some 200 gladiators, mainly Thracians and Gauls, resentful of their inhumane treatment in the gladiatorial training school of Cnaeus Lentulus Batiatus, hatched a plan to escape. The leaders were the Thracian Spartacus and the Gauls Crixus and Oenomaus.

It all started in the mess hall. This was the place where the gladiators gathered to eat, at one end of which was the kitchen and the other a pair of heavy wooden doors. Once the gladiators were inside, these doors were bolted from the outside. Having taken their places, the gladiators would then be served by the kitchen slaves, women in the main. Patrolling the mess hall were guards armed with hefty batons.

Armed with cleavers and spits seized from the kitchen, they overpowered the guards and fought their way to freedom. As they raced through the streets of Capua they found a cart loaded with gladiatorial weapons and equipment, which they also seized. Once out of the city and having driven off the detachment of troops (possibly local militia) sent after them, Spartacus and

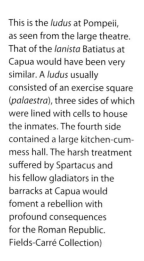

This is the *ludus* at Pompeii, as seen from the large theatre. That of the *lanista* Batiatus at Capua would have been very similar. A *ludus* usually consisted of an exercise square (*palaestra*), three sides of which were lined with cells to house the inmates. The fourth side contained a large kitchen-cum-mess hall. The harsh treatment suffered by Spartacus and his fellow gladiators in the barracks at Capua would foment a rebellion with profound consequences for the Roman Republic. Fields-Carré Collection)

the other gladiators sought refuge on the slopes of nearby Mount Vesuvius, then dormant and believed to be extinct.

Fewer than half seem to have succeeded – '80 lacking two' in Plutarch (*Crassus* 8.2); 74 in Sallust (*Historiae* 3.90), Livy (*Periochae* 95), Frontinus (*Strategemata* 1.5.21), Orosius (5.24.1), and Eutropius (6.7.2); 'about 70' in Appian (*Bellum civilia* 1.116); 'fewer than 70' in Augustine (*City of God* 3.26); 64 in Velleius Paterculus (*Historiae Romanae* 2.30.5); no more than 50 (taken at face value) in Cicero (*Epistulae ad Atticum* 6.2.8); and '30 or rather more men' in Florus (*Epitome* 3.20.3). Although the number of fugitive-gladiators is variously reported, the important point is the sources' agreement that the beginnings of the rebellion involved but a handful of desperate individuals.

DEFEAT OF THE PRAETORIAN ARMIES, 73 BC

In the crater of Mount Vesuvius Spartacus quickly forged an army of runaway slaves and free people with little to lose, and defeated the troops – 'forces picked up in haste and at random' (Appian *Bellum civilia* 1.116) – under one of the praetors of 73 BC Caius Claudius Glaber (*MMR* II.109), sent to besiege the rebels' volcanic fastness. A brave man asleep is but an infant, and the victorious rebels seized the Roman camp with all its possessions and supplies. Never was a military expedition more certain of failure, and its fate throws into relief the cast-iron prejudices of the Roman ruling order.

Mount Vesuvius (1,281m), though clearly volcanic, was reputed extinct (Strabo 5.247). After the catastrophic eruption of 24 August AD 79, which obliterated Pompeii and Herculaneum, the sides of Vesuvius caved in to form an immense crater some 11km in circumference. The north-eastern side of this old crater still exists, but a new cone has formed on the south side. This photograph shows the eruption that took place on the afternoon of 26 April 1872. (Library of Congress)

Meanwhile, in Rome the Senate were still looking upon the slave rebellion as little more than an irritant that would be soothed in due course, and so two more praetors for that year were sent south to clean up this trouble and restore order. The praetors, Lucius Cossinius (*MMR* II.110) and Publius Varinius (*MMR* II.109, 119), as well as Varinius' legate Furius (Caius or Lucius, cf. *MMR* II.112) and his quaestor Caius Toranius (*MMR* II.110), all suffered thundering defeats in separate encounters. Furius, who commanded 2,000 men, was seen off with little trouble. Cossinius first narrowly escaped capture while taking a bath, only to die a short while later in an engagement over his own camp. When Varinius managed to surround his camp, Spartacus stole his army away at night, having created the impression that all was normal. But the sentries posted, properly clothed and armed, were in fact fresh corpses lashed to stakes, whose object, together with the evening fires that had been left burning throughout the camp, was to provide cover for the rebels' silent withdrawal. The Romans were indeed fooled and only noticed something was amiss when they missed the customary insults shouted across at them, and the shower of stones that normally greeted them at sunup (Sallust *Historiae* 3.96, Frontinus *Strategemata* 1.5.22).

Varinius was to fight several engagements with Spartacus, and he lost each and every one of them. Most ignominiously, in the last of these the praetor had his very horse and six lictors captured, in other words, all the insignia of his office fell into the victor's hands. There was a cost, of course, and sometime during these events Oenomaus, who now disappears from the pages of our sources, may have been killed in battle. Even so, these stunning victories encouraged many a malcontent to flock to join Spartacus, as did 'many of the herdsmen and shepherds of the surrounding regions – hard-bodied and swift-footed men' (Plutarch *Crassus* 9.3). Spartacus spent the winter training and arming his new recruits.

Spartacus had ropes and ladders made from wild vines and with his men climbed down the volcano to the rear of the besieging Romans. This wall painting (Naples, Museo Archeologico Nazionale) from the House of the Centenary, Pompeii, shows a verdant Vesuvius. Indeed, at the time the upper slopes of the volcano were densely wooded, while those lower down were cultivated with olive groves and vineyards. (Fields-Carré Collection)

DEFEAT OF THE CONSULAR ARMIES, 72 BC

The following spring, with an army reputed by Appian (*Bellum civilia* 1.116) to be some 70,000 strong, Spartacus swept through Campania, with specific assaults on the prosperous towns of Cumae, Nola, and Nuceria, the rebels leaving a thick trail of dead men, women and livestock and burning villas in their wake. There is also evidence that the rebellion now affected Lucania and Bruttium, the latter a region long associated with chronic brigandage, with the towns of Thurii (Sibari), Metapontum (Metaponto) and Cosentia (Cosenza) as objects of eventual attack. Spartacus tried to restrain the worse of this barbarity, but a perilous division in the high command had resulted in his comrade Crixus departing, taking the Gauls and Germans with him, a force of about 20,000 or thereabouts (Plutarch *Crassus* 9.6, Livy *Periochae* 96).

The sparse, denuded slopes of Mount Vesuvius, captured in a late 19th-century photograph. To those who lived around Vesuvius in Spartacus' day, the volcano was just a large, lush mound. Its last eruption had been a thousand years in the past, and its next was to be some 150 years in the future. It has erupted many times since that date, and any plants, shrubs or trees growing on it have been burnt away or swallowed by lava. (Library of Congress)

Like his comrade Spartacus, Crixus the Gaul had been trained as a gladiator in the school of Batiatus. Towards the end of 73 BC he was to separate from Spartacus, it seems, over matter of policy. While Spartacus wanted to head north and leave Italy, 'Crixus and his people', in the words of Sallust, 'wanted to march directly against the enemy, in order to force an armed confrontation' (*Historiae* 3.96). And so it was in the spring of 72 BC that one of the two consuls for the year, Lucius Gellius Publicola, caught up with Crixus and his followers near Mount Garganus, on the Adriatic coast.

The numbers involved in the ensuing battle were, as is usually the case, the subject of some controversy. Though Appian (*Bellum civilia* 1.116) puts Crixus' army at 30,000 strong, Livy, an earlier source albeit here in the form of a later summary, gives him only 20,000 followers. Sallust, in the aforementioned fragment, identifies Crixus' people as Gauls and Germans, while Plutarch names neither Crixus nor gives the size of his following, merely calling them 'the German contingent' (*Crassus* 9.7). If the truth be known, Crixus led not an army, but a whole travelling people – warriors, women, waifs, and wagons. On the other hand, it is almost certain that the Romans had some 10,000 men, what we would expect of a consular army of two, full-strength legions.

Despite their tatterdemalion appearance, the rebels of Crixus' army put up a savage fight. Apparently, if we follow the fragmentary Sallust, Gellius 'ordered his men to form a double battle line on a commanding height of land and defended it, but with heavy losses to his own forces' (*Historiae* 3.106). The rebels were obviously the attackers, and the fact that the defenders deployed in a *duplex acies*, each legion presumably in a five–five formation of cohorts, instead of the more usual *triplex acies*, meant the Romans were heavily outnumbered. But we have no more than this. Perhaps, and in any case it is impossible at this distance in time to do anything other than speculate about the course of the battle. We can guess that the rebels climbed up the steep hillside against the disciplined Romans only to be bounced back down again. The second attack was likewise repulsed, as was the third and the fourth. The attackers hesitated, turned, and fled, and the pursuing swords

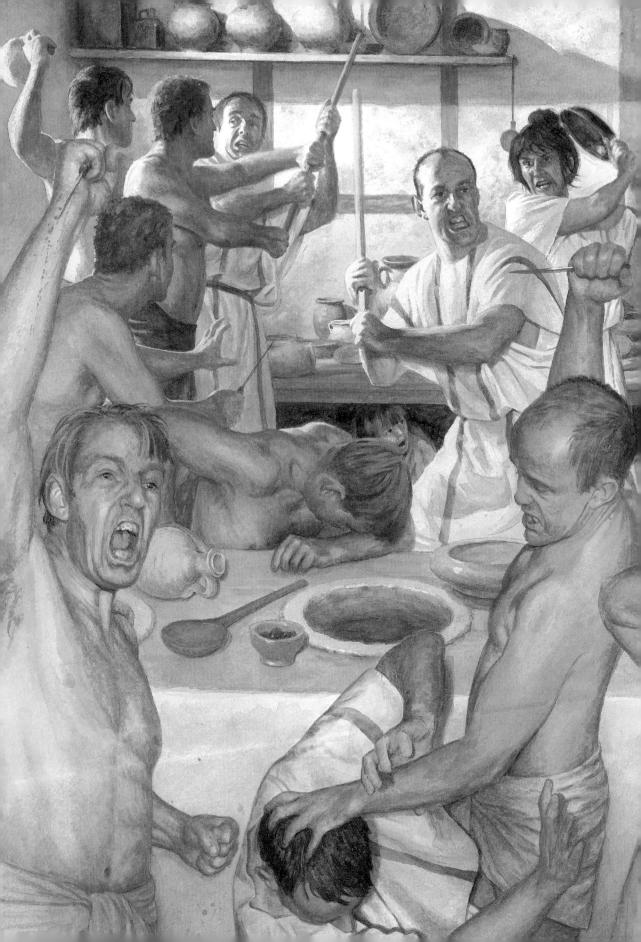

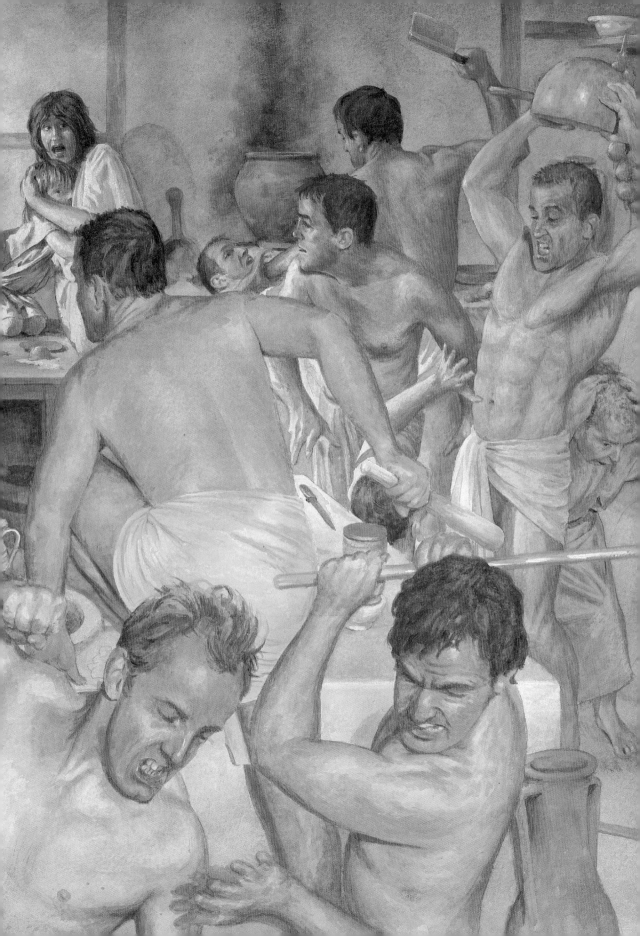

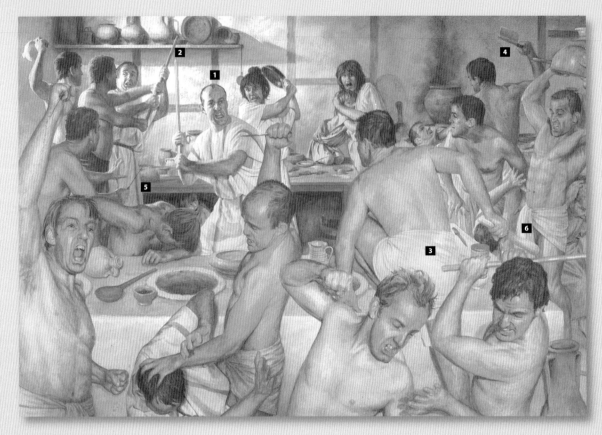

BREAKOUT AT CAPUA (pp 56–57)

Since the purpose of a *ludus* was to produce prime prize-fighters, it was in the interest of the *lanista* to maintain his gladiators at the peak of physical condition. Thus, there was a kitchen staff charged with preparing wholesome meals for the gladiators. High in protein and fat, barley groats (*polenta*) made into a gruel, was the mainstay of the diet, a food believed to be healthy and muscle promoting. Gladiators were commonly known as as *hordearii*, 'barley-men', which reflected the cereal's benefits in furnishing a good layer of fat that helped prevent heavy bleeding if vital arteries were sliced in combat.

This plate depicts the moment when the group of some 200 gladiators, mainly Thracians and Gauls, resentful of their owner's inhumane treatment, executed their plan to escape. The chaotic scene is set in the kitchen end of the mess hall at the gladiatorial training school of Cnaeus Lentulus Batiatus in Capua. The gladiators are overpowering the guards **(1)**, who are armed with batons **(2)**; this was all done to great effect in Kubrick's epic film *Spartacus* of course, with a lengthy scene (cut in the original) of a man being drowned in a pot of piping-hot soup. Except for loincloths **(3)**, the gladiators are naked; they are clean shaven and their hair is cut short. From the kitchen they grab everything that can service as weapons, the knives and cleavers **(4)** and spits **(5)**, and even the heavy, wooden pestles **(6)** used for grinding the grain for the daily porridge. And so it was the gladiators hacked and beat their way out of the school of Batiatus, and then fled in the direction of Mount Vesuvius.

were not far behind. After that Crixus' command ceased to exist; we shall assume that the fiercely moustached Crixus, seeking death out on the battlefield, went down fighting. Such was the carnage at Garganus.

Plutarch hints that the generalship of Gellius was open to reproach; the high reputation gained in this campaign by the younger Cato, who had volunteered for service against Spartacus out of devotion to his older half-brother, Quintus Servilius Caepio, then serving as a military tribune in the consul's army, formed at least a signal contrast to the elderly Gellius' half-hearted bungling. Cato, no way inferior to the great ancestor whom he emulated almost to a parody, Cato the Elder, extolled the so-called simplicity and virtues that won empire for Rome in times past despite, in Plutarch's stinging words, 'the effeminacy and laxity of those who fought in the war' (*Cato minor* 8.2).

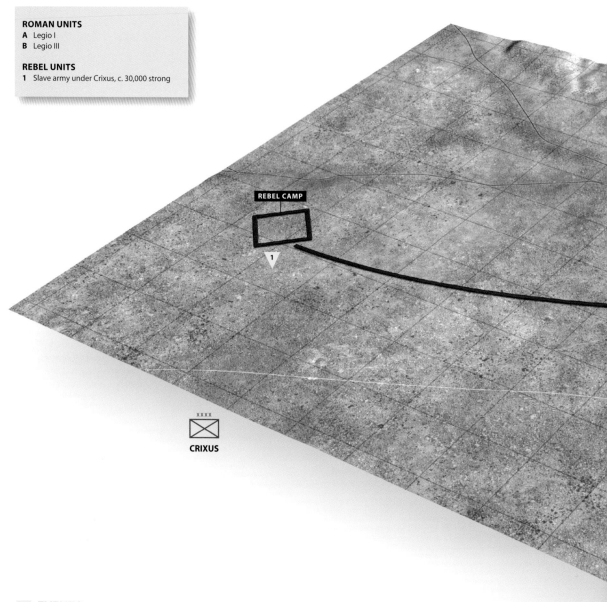

ROMAN UNITS
A Legio I
B Legio III

REBEL UNITS
1 Slave army under Crixus, c. 30,000 strong

REBEL CAMP

1

XXXX
CRIXUS

▼ **EVENTS**

1 Having split off from the main slave army, Crixus and his followers are now encamped in the vicinity of Mount Garganus in north-eastern Apulia.

2 Lucius Gellius Publicola has caught up with Crixus, but being outnumbered decides to deploy his two consular legions on high ground in *duplex acies*, each legion adopting in a five–five formation of cohorts.

3 Crixus responds the way he knows best, and promptly marshals his Gauls and Germans for the attack.

4 Crixus leads his men up the steep hill in three successive assaults on the Roman position. The fourth and final one results in Crixus' death and the destruction of his army.

MOUNT GARGANUS, 72 BC

Crixus' slave army is destroyed in the vicinity of Mount Garganus, in south-eastern Italy, by the pursuing consular legions under Lucius Gellius Publicola.

Note: the gridlines are shown at intervals of 1km/1,093 yds

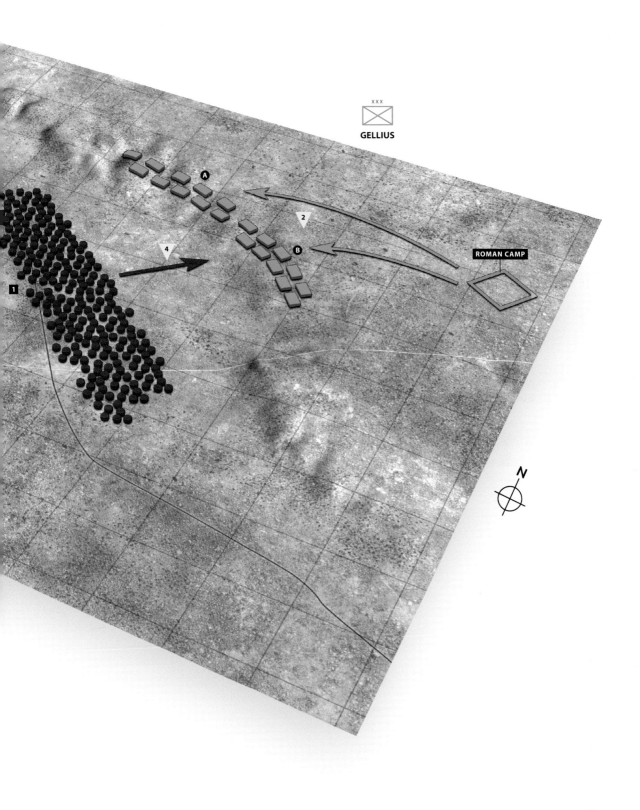

GELLIUS

A

ROMAN CAMP

B

1

2

4

N

61

Seating and orchestra of the Greek theatre at Metapontum (Metaponto). Sometime in the early part of 72 BC, and before he trekked north to the River Po, Spartacus, like Hannibal before him, used Metapontum as a friendly base. As well as securing supplies for his army and gathering its strength, he would have trained recently arrived recruits in the relative security of the town. (Fototeca ENIT)

Meanwhile, Cnaeus Cornelius Lentulus Clodianus, the other consul, attempted to harry Spartacus as he headed north. Spartacus, however, seized the initiative and turned on the Romans before they could join forces and smashed both consuls in turn, who were consequently recalled to Rome in disgrace and promptly relieved of their duties by the infuriated Senate (Plutarch *Crassus* 10.1). The presence of armies of different consuls clearly raised all the political and operational difficulties of divided command. As Napoleon would later have it, 'one bad general would be better than two good ones' (*Correspondance*, vol. I, no. 421). However, considering the Senate's (unusual) reaction, in this particular case it seems we are dealing with two bad generals up against a brilliant one.

Appian (*Bellum civilia* 1.117) tells how, in mockery of the Roman custom, Spartacus now forced 300 of his Roman prisoners to fight as gladiators, killing their own comrades to save their own lives, to appease the spirit of dead Crixus. Thus, in the rather fitting phrase of Orosius, 'those who had once been the spectacle became the spectators' (5.24.4). Clearly the Thracian had a cruel sense of irony.

Moving north again, Spartacus' intention, according to Plutarch (*Crassus* 9.5), was to cross the Alps into Gaul and then to Thrace. Outside Mutina (Modena) on the plain of the River Po he defeated Caius Cassius Longinus (*cos.* 73 BC), the governor of Gallia Cisalpina and general of an army of two legions. The proconsul was nearly killed but escaped with difficulty. The road to the Alpine passes was open and the prospects looked promising. At this point Spartacus changes his mind, and for some inexplicable reason he turned back and headed south again. At one juncture he contemplated attacking Rome, yet in the event he returned to the south of the peninsula and eventually spent the winter near Thurii instead (Appian *Bellum civilia* 1.117).

Spartacus now posed an enormous (and embarrassing) threat to Rome. He and his slave army had shredded the armies of three praetors, two consuls and one proconsul with apparent ease. The rebellion had become war, and war to the bitter end.

THE WAR WITH CRASSUS, 71 BC

Marcus Licinius Crassus, who had been praetor in the previous year, was given 10 legions, six of them newly raised and the rest taken over from the disgraced consuls, and entrusted with the overall command of the war against Spartacus. As the rebels were making their way south, Crassus took up a position in the region of Picenum (present-day Marches) and ordered his legate Mummius to shadow but not to engage Spartacus. When an opportunity presented itself, he disobeyed the order and attacked; his two legions were trounced, and reportedly a large number of the troops ran from the battlefield. In turn, Spartacus retreated across Lucania to the sea.

Violence, especially in war, is a confused and uncertain activity, highly unpredictable and depending on decisions taken by fallible human beings. It is furthermore a hot-headed activity in which commitments and reputations can develop a momentum of their own. Crassus must have feared his opponent, for instead of forcing a decisive battle he planned to trap Spartacus in the toe of Italy by means of an immense trench that stretched 'from sea to sea, across the narrow neck of land, for a length of three hundred stades' (*c.* 60km, Plutarch *Crassus* 10.5). Crassus then had a low earth rampart, topped with a palisade and studded with turrets, thrown up along its entire length.

Gargano hills of Promontorio del Gargano, ancient Mount Garganus. It was somewhere in the shadow of these hills that Crixus and his followers, Gauls and Germans in the main, met their untimely end. Their nemesis was one of the consular armies, that of Gellius. Despite his advanced years (he was in his sixties), the consul stubbornly held his own by deploying his two legions on high ground. (APT Puglia)

Spartacus' movements, spring 71 BC

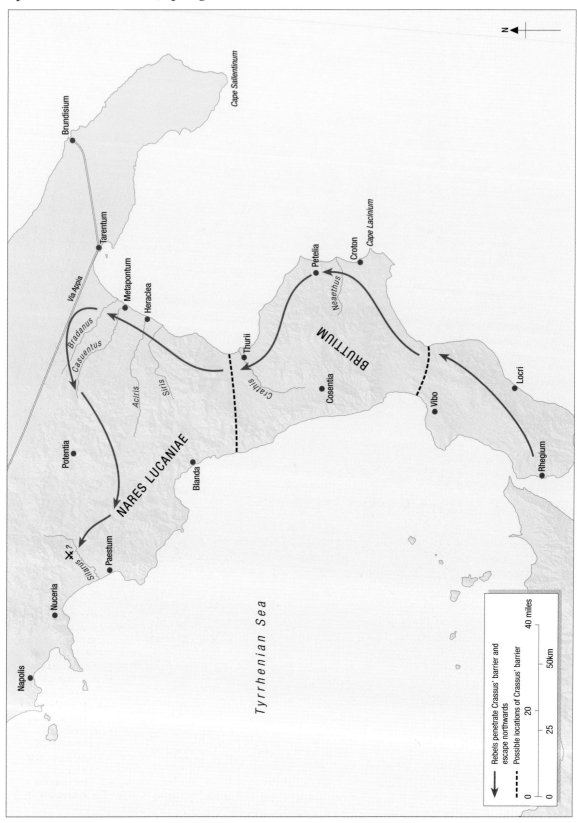

It has been doubted by some that the trench stretched for the 300 stades that Plutarch claims. Ward (1977: 89-90 n. 20), for instance, suggests that Spartacus was encamped on the Scyllaeum promontory, just north of Rhegium (Reggio di Calabria) and overlooking the strait separating Italy from Sicily, and that Crassus dug a trench that traversed this promontory and not the whole toe of Italy. It is true that Spartacus had hoped that Cilician pirates would transport him and his men across the narrow but treacherous strait to the island – the Second Slave War had not long ended and could easily be rekindled – yet in the event they took the money and sailed off. Besides, Plutarch is quite specific in the details of length and a fragment of Sallust, the

TOP

Like its northern neighbour Lucania, Bruttium (present-day Calabria) was a mountainous region whose economy was chiefly based on livestock breeding and the use of the forests. It was considered by the Romans as a wilderness where decent people hardly dare venture and where bandits abound. In the 19th century the region was still the scene of acts of banditry. A view of Largo Arvo, Calabria. (Fototeca ENIT)

RIGHT

An oft-forgotten achievement of Crassus was the fortification, some 60km long, which he had constructed across the toe of Italy to bottle up the slave army. Pinpointing the actual course of this barrier, however, is an exercise in conjecture. This is the Calabrian seaside town of Pizzo, on Golfo di Santa Eufemia, a possible candidate for its western terminal. (Fototeca ENIT)

possible source here, tantalizingly mentions 'that part of Italy that stretches out in the direction of Sicily is entered by a corridor that is no wider than thirty-five [Roman] miles' (*c.* 52km, *Historiae* 4.25). Such patient feats of military engineering were well within the capabilities of the army of the Republic and, by way of a comparison, the stone wall of contravallation and accompanying ditch that sealed off Numantia from the outside world, constructed some 60 years earlier, ran for a total distance of 48 stades (*c.* 10km, Appian *Iberica* 90). In any event, Spartacus and his army were certainly cut off from the more succulent lands to the north, and from now on would have to endure much and live on little. The rebels were indeed caught in a rat trap.

It was normal of course for any ancient army to live off the land in wartime conditions, or else to exact appropriations from local communities too powerless to resist, and with the rebels moving from one locale to another,

windfall acquisitions must have made up a large part of requirements. Herdsmen used to habitually living off the country would obviously have known what to take for their immediate needs, but for the rest of the army it was a different matter. Caesar would later say that war could feed war, and he was right; the corresponding French axiom *la guerre nourrit la guerre* can also be found in Napoleon's writings (e.g. *Correspondance*, vol. I, no. 49). Moreover, as the war grew into long campaigns during difficult winter months, a more efficient method of providing provisions was desirable in order to complement the gains of simple plundering.

DESTRUCTION OF CRIXUS (pp 68–69)

Towards the end of 73 BC Crixus and his followers separated from Spartacus. The following spring he and his entire force were destroyed near Mount Garganus (Promontorio del Gargano) in north-eastern Apulia after being compromised by one of the two consular armies sent to quash the slave rebellion, that of Lucius Gellius Publicola. It is of interest to note here that in Kubrick's *Spartacus*, contrary to ancient sources, Crixus is always portrayed as Spartacus' loyal lieutenant, right up to the famous scene after the final battle when he is one of the first to stand up and call out, 'I am Spartacus!'

This illustration shows the moment of the third (penultimate) attack by Crixus' army. The rebels are beginning their slow ascent of the hill, atop of which stand the waiting Romans. Crixus **(1)**, on foot and looking very much the Gaulish warlord, is prominent in front; the elderly Gellius **(2)** who was about 64 years old, on horseback, is slightly to the rear of the Roman (double) battle line. The steep hillside is strewn with the dead and the dying. Crixus' followers are mainly Gauls **(3)** or Germans **(4)**, some sporting their native style of dress and weaponry, others in a *mélange* of native and Roman equipment, yet others looking more like herdsmen **(5)** than warriors. A few women **(6)** combatants are evident too.

'The Pledge of Spartacus', marble statue group in the neoclassical style by Louis-Ernest Barrias, Jardin des Tuileries, Paris. Both Sallust (*Historiae* 3.91) and Plutarch (*Crassus* 8.2) praise the great bodily strength and spirit of Spartacus, but here we view the rebel gladiator in defeat. Executed in 1871, Barrias' sculpture obviously symbolizes the tumultuous political events that had just shattered Paris, the glittering capital of Europe. (Ancient Art & Architecture)

In spite of these reverses, however, one wild, wintry night, with snow falling on the ground, Spartacus and a portion of his slave army managed to penetrate Crassus' makeshift barrier by filling a section of the trench with both materials (earth, wood, branches) and carrion (human, cattle, and horse). Again Spartacus was soon at large in the open country of the mainland. Again Crassus pursued. No mention is made in our sources of the fate of those who did not break out, though it is possible that these were the rebels under the command of Castus and Gannicus – leaders previously unheard of – who fell victim to a surprise attack (Plutarch *Crassus* 11.2–3, Frontinus *Strategemata* 1.5.20, 2.4.7, 5.34, Orosius 5.24.6).

THE TRAP CLOSES: RIVER SILARUS, 71 BC

Meanwhile the Senate, becoming impatient, called upon Pompey, who with his veteran legions was returning home by land from Iberia, and Marcus

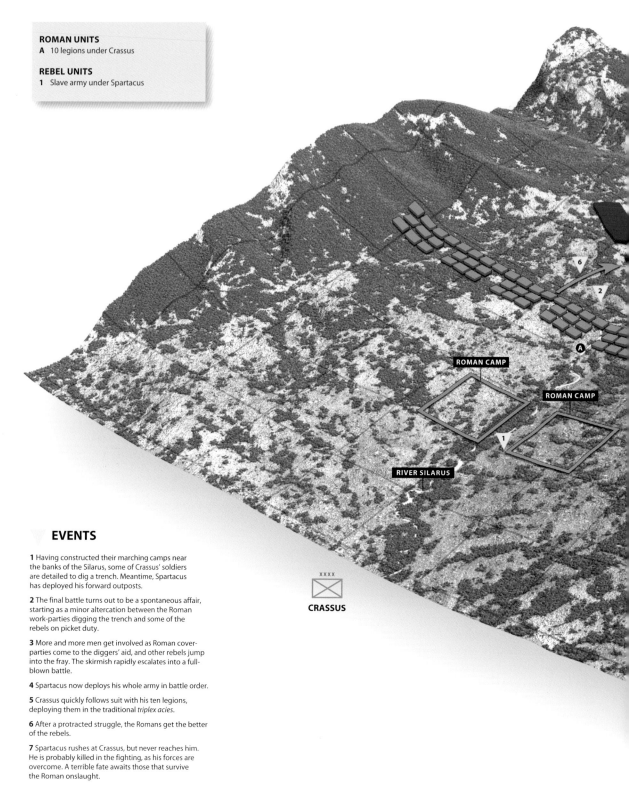

ROMAN UNITS
A 10 legions under Crassus

REBEL UNITS
1 Slave army under Spartacus

ROMAN CAMP

ROMAN CAMP

RIVER SILARUS

xxxx
CRASSUS

EVENTS

1 Having constructed their marching camps near the banks of the Silarus, some of Crassus' soldiers are detailed to dig a trench. Meantime, Spartacus has deployed his forward outposts.

2 The final battle turns out to be a spontaneous affair, starting as a minor altercation between the Roman work-parties digging the trench and some of the rebels on picket duty.

3 More and more men get involved as Roman cover-parties come to the diggers' aid, and other rebels jump into the fray. The skirmish rapidly escalates into a full-blown battle.

4 Spartacus now deploys his whole army in battle order.

5 Crassus quickly follows suit with his ten legions, deploying them in the traditional *triplex acies*.

6 After a protracted struggle, the Romans get the better of the rebels.

7 Spartacus rushes at Crassus, but never reaches him. He is probably killed in the fighting, as his forces are overcome. A terrible fate awaits those that survive the Roman onslaught.

THE SILARUS RIVER, 71 BC

Spartacus' forces are annihilated by Marcus Licinius Crassus in the upper reaches of the Silarus (Sele) River in south-western Italy, bringing the slave rebellion to an end.

xxxx

SPARTACUS

EL CAMP

1

7

The Sele (Silarus) originates from Monte Paflagone, Monti Picentini range, just above Calabritto, and flows into the Golfo di Salerno in the Tyrrhenian Sea just north of Paestum, a length of some 64km. Its main tributaries are the Tanagro (Tanagrus) and the Calore (Calor), which join it from the south. It was somewhere along the Sele, probably near its source, that Spartacus fought his final battle. (Fototeca ENIT)

Terentius Varro Lucullus (*cos.* 73 BC), the younger of the two Luculli and proconsul of Macedonia, to assist Crassus in terminating the war. On learning of this, Spartacus set out for Brundisium (Brindisi) in order to escape by sea to Epeiros, but when he discovered the port was garrisoned, probably with the soldiers of Lucullus, he abandoned the attempt. The sands of time were running out. Crassus was far away, but he was steadily closing the distance between himself and Spartacus. After a series of escalating clashes, Spartacus was finally brought to heel in north-western Lucania by the dogged Crassus. At his back, for both political and personal reasons, Crassus must have heard time's winged chariot hovering near.

It takes little effort for us to imagine a Crassus who would have begun to fear Pompey's return, a move that would steal his thunder. Sometime in the spring of 71 BC a major battle was fought near the source of the River Silarus (Sele) in north-western Lucania, and Spartacus was defeated and slain. The words of Plutarch provide us with one version of the final moments of this heroic figure:

Slingshot (Paestum, Museo Archeologico) found under the pavement of the Basilica at Paestum. Believed to date to the time of the Spartacan rebellion, these examples are of baked clay. Such purpose-made projectiles allowed a very high consistency of size and shape that would aid range and accuracy. Of course they were easy to mass-produce in large quantities too. (Fields-Carré Collection)

Then pushing his way towards Crassus himself, through many flying weapons and wounded men, he did not indeed reach him, but slew two centurions who fell upon him together. Finally, after his companions had taken to flight, he stood alone, surrounded by a multitude of foes, and was still defending himself when he was cut down. (Plutarch *Crassus* 11.6–7)

And so perished the heroic gladiator, eventually defeated but never disgraced. As Appian notes, 'The body of Spartacus was never found' (*Bellum civilia* 1.120). Of course, it can be argued that if the body was never found there is no proof that Spartacus did not survive the carnage. But what of the price of this carnage and the ugliness connected with it?

In all probability, along with Spartacus, 60,000 of his followers were slain that fateful day, while the Roman losses amounted to about 1,000 men (Livy *Periochae* 97, Appian *Bellum civilia* 1.120). Yet victory had its own price too; three years of devastation, especially in the south, and 50,000 additional recruits levied to help quash the rebellion. All this on top of a butcher's bill that included, as far as we can tell, 150,000 among the servile population of the peninsula and thousands of Romans (Brunt 1988: 107). The conflict had dispatched countless people, rebel survivors and peasants alike, who presumably resorted to banditry, the only alternative in poor preindustrial societies, though for the free poor there was always the option of joining the army.

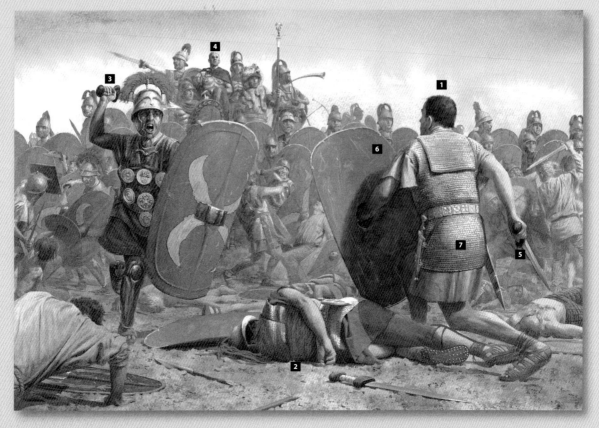

SPARTACUS RUSHES AT CRASSUS (pp 76–77)

And so it came about, in the springtime of 71 BC, that Spartacus died on his feet fighting, surrounded by Romans. Not far away was a grassy knoll whereupon Crassus stood and watched.

On that fateful day instead of meeting the enemy on horseback, Spartacus refused to mount his horse, a symbol of aristocratic generalship, when it was led up to him. Dramatically proclaiming that he would have plenty of horses to ride if he won and no need of one if he lost, he then plunged his sword into the magnificent animal. Then, bloody sword in hand, he plunged fearlessly into the fray on foot and almost cut his way to Crassus before he was cut down. He did, however, kill two centurions that came to Crassus' rescue. He died not as a general of an army,

but as a gladiator in an arena. Thus ended the battle by the River Silarus, when the Spartacan rebellion went down into the dust of Roman history.

This illustration, in some respects, is reminiscent of a scene from the arena. Spartacus **(1)** has just cut down one of the centurions **(2)** and is about to engage the second **(3)**. In the background, much like a spectator at the Roman games, stands Crassus **(4)**. Meanwhile round and about, almost a blur in fact, rages the final battle between the slaves and the masters. As for Spartacus' arms and armour, he wields the *gladius* **(5)** and *scutum* **(6)** of an ordinary Roman legionary, and likewise wears a legionary's mail shirt, the *lorica hamata* **(7)**. He is bareheaded and battle scarred.

AFTERMATH

The Via Appia, called by the poet Statius (*Silvae* 4.3) the *regina viarum*, was begun during the censorship of Appius Claudius Caecus (312 BC), making it easy for Roman troops to move between Rome and the new conquest of Capua. Following the approximate line of an earlier trackway to the Alban hills at Bovillae, it was paved with basalt from the Porta Capena, a gate in the Servian wall near the Circus Maximus, to the temple of Mars, the initial *mille passus* or Roman mile (296 BC), then all the way to Bovillae (293 BC), and subsequently extended across the malaria-infested *paludes Pomptinae*, the mountains between Fundi and Formiae, and the *ager Campanus*, thus running a total of 132 Roman miles to Capua. A further 32-mile extension would take it on to Beneventum, the road passing near the notorious defile of Caudium, site of the battle of the Caudine Forks (321 BC), and thence by Venusia to Tarentum, thereby adding another 202 Roman miles, and finally Brundisium.

An important aspect of Rome's absorption of conquered territory was to construct roads linking new colonies to Rome. In Italy itself, as the Via Appia ideally illustrates, the major arterial roads tended to follow Rome's conquests both in time and space. Yet Rome's first great highway, the 'Queen of Roads' herself, was about to become the route of the damned.

CRUCIFIXION

With Spartacus dead, the remnants of his slave army were quickly hunted down and terrible examples made of them. Roman law sanctioned the most brutal of death penalties, the *summa supplica* – throwing to the beasts, burning alive, and crucifixion – as savageries that were necessary 'to set a public example' (*Digesta* 48.19.16.10). Crucifixion, which went back well into the early years of the Republic, was an aggravated capital punishment closely connected with the dual and interrelated threats of servile rebellion and banditry. Used earlier in the Near East and probably devised in Persia, crucifixion at Rome seems to have developed from a form of punishment (the public carrying of a cross, being bound to it, and whipped) to a form of execution (being attached to a cross and suspended).

Victims of crucifixion died slow, agonizing deaths, and they were guarded. Usually, to prolong the message of deterrence, corpses were then simply left to suffer consumption by carrion birds, wild animals and natural decomposition. Each step of crucifixion was designed to be, in every sense of the term, excruciating (Latin *excruciatus*, literally 'out of the crucified'). Hung from nails

The Via Appia, which connected Rome with Campania, Lucania and Apulia, was the first and most spectacular of the consular roads. As far as Terracina, a distance of 62 Roman miles, it ran in an almost entirely straight line, even through the Alban Hills, where the gradients are steep. Here we see the well-paved stretch just beyond the Tomb of Cecilia Metella, Parco Regionale dell'Appia Antica. (Fields-Carré Collection)

the victim would suffer in the extreme, eventually dying with fractured limbs and blackened tongue. For exemplary effect, crucifixions were held at well-travelled public roadways, offering a stark contrast to the hallowed burials of good citizens nearby.

Crucifixion was Crassus' choice of punishment. He ordered a row of wooden crosses to be set up on either side of the Via Appia, lining the 132-mile route of his march from Capua, where the rebellion had begun, to the very gates of Rome, as a gruesome warning to everybody passing along it. The 6,000 rebel slaves would hang at regular intervals in an uninterrupted sequence.

The agonizing process for each of the rebels would no doubt have been the same. The cross for each rebel, hurriedly hewn out of fresh new pine, was placed on the ground. The rebel was quickly thrown backwards with his shoulders against the rough wood of the *patibulum*, a horizontal beam attached to the vertical beam that would soon be set in the ground. A Roman soldier felt for the depression at the front of the rebel's wrist, before forcefully driving a heavy, square wrought-iron nail some 12–18cm long through the man's flesh deep into the soft wood. The soldier would then move quickly to the other side and repeat the process, being careful not pull the arms too tightly, but to allow some flex and movement. The cross was then raised slightly. The left foot of the rebel was pressed backwards against his right, and with both feet extended, toes down, a nail would be driven through the arch of each into the vertical beam, leaving the knees flexed. The cross was then fully raised and set into the ground.

As he slowly sagged down, more of the rebel's weight was placed on the nails piercing the wrists, causing excruciating pain to shoot along the fingers and up the arm. As he pushed himself upward to avoid this torment, he would place his full weight on the nail piercing his feet. Again he would feel the searing agony of the nail tearing through flesh and bone. As the arms tired, cramps would sweep through his muscles, causing them to knot. With these cramps came the inability to push himself upwards to breathe. Air could be drawn into the lungs, but not exhaled. He would fight to raise himself in order to catch one small breath. As carbon dioxide accumulated in his bloodstream, the cramps would partially subside. Spasmodically, he would be able to push himself upward to exhale and gain oxygen. Hours of pain, cycles of cramps, intermittent asphyxiation lay ahead. Then another torment would begin: crushing pain in the chest as the pericardium slowly filled with fluid and began to compress the heart. The loss of bodily fluids would reach a critical level, the heart struggling to pump torpid blood, and the lungs making frantic efforts to function. The rebel would now be feeling the chill of death.

The journey home from Capua for Crassus and his troops was to be a spectacle the like of which had never been seen before. Their return was intended to be one long triumphal procession. It is simple to say that the punishment fits the crime, but the deliberate cruelties of property and privilege are invariably more fiendish than the hot-headed revenges of poverty and oppression; Crassus' prisoners died horribly.

In addition to the 6,000 rebels crucified by Crassus, another 5,000 of Spartacus' followers, as they attempted to flee northwards, fell in with Pompey, who promptly exterminated every last one. Pompey, always one to take his own charm and authority for granted, then penned a brief dispatch to the Senate, claiming 'that although Crassus had defeated the gladiators in a pitched battle, he had extinguished the war to its very roots' (Plutarch *Pompey* 21.5). Pompey's self-promotion helped to make him a popular hero. Crassus' hurt can only be imagined.

Early 11th-century mosaic on a gold ground, narthex of katholikon, Osios Loukás Monastry showing 'Jesus Christ and Him crucified'. A foot support has been added to prolong the ordeal. The nails are shown piercing the hands, not the wrist as per normal practice, while each foot is nailed as opposed to the feet being nailed one on top of the other. (Fields-Carré Collection)

THE RETURN TO ORDER

The armies of Crassus and Pompey converged on Rome in a mood of mutual hostility, yet both men looked for a consulship and to gain it each needed the support of the other. Crassus' assets were that he was fabulously rich, and numerous senators were indebted to him; Pompey's that he was the idol of the people. So they set their differences aside, provisionally linked arms, and were duly elected to the consulships for the following year. They then disbanded their war-weary veterans. On the pretext that they were awaiting their triumphs, the pair had maintained their armies and then had menacingly pitched up at the very gates of the capital.

We should not overlook the fact that Pompey received a triumph for defeating Sertorius in Iberia. This was rather irregular as Sertorius had been a Roman citizen and Pompey had yet to hold public office and enter the Senate, both of which he was to do on 29 December 71 BC, the very day he rode in glorious triumph along the Via Sacra. The legitimate Crassus, on the other hand, was only voted a lesser triumph, an *ovatio* or ovation, as the vanquishing of Spartacus and his slave army was not considered worthy of the full glory of a full-scale triumph. In the second-rate victory parade, however, he did wear a crown of laurel rather than the customary myrtle, which may have been regarded as a special distinction for the otherwise bitterly disappointed Crassus (Cicero *In Pisonem* 58, Pliny *Historia Naturalis* 15.125, Plutarch *Crassus* 11.8, Aulus Gellius *Noctes Atticae* 5.6.23).

As for their year of cooperation, unsurprisingly vanities clashed. Pompey, conceited and unscrupulous, tried to treat Crassus like a junior colleague, as the apprentice to the sorcerer he expected admiration and deference. Whereas Crassus, conceited and superior, would look down on Pompey as his social inferior, little more than a vulgar parvenu (Sallust *Historiae* 4.48, Plutarch *Crassus* 12, *Pompey* 22).

One more question remains to be answered, in truth the most realistic and most pregnant question of all: did Spartacus' rebellion ever have the slightest chance of success? It is possible to argue that, at least initially, not enough slaves had joined Spartacus to make his victory possible. At one point or another, Spartacus must have realized that the masses of slaves who toiled in Italy would not or could not rise up and join him, and, much like Hannibal before him, no matter how many times he knocked out a Roman army, another would stubbornly take its place. As the cinematic Spartacus says to his wife Varinia, 'no matter how many times we beat them, they always seem to have another army to send against us. And another.'

Also, extreme measures to preserve unity might have been the only way to keep the chances for future victory alive. Any breakaway movements by portions of the slave army would almost inevitably lead to disaster, as it ultimately did. In an army, no subordination no discipline, and no discipline no army. Of course, it is the privilege of historians to be wise after the event, and the more foolish the historian the wiser he usually aims to be.

Reverberations of the war continued after the final defeat of Spartacus. During the Catilinarian crisis of 63 BC the Senate decreed the troupes of gladiators in Rome were to be removed to Capua and other Campanian towns in order to relieve the capital of the potential dangers their presence represented. In 49 BC, as civil war began, Caesar had 5,000 gladiators located in Capua, a body that the Pompeian consul Lucius Cornelius Lentulus contemplated using as troops but whose members were, in the words of Cicero, 'very sensibly distributed by Pompey among the population, two per household'(*Epistulae ad Atticum* 7.14.2).

Some survivors from the Spartacan rebellion even managed to remain at large for nigh on a decade after Crassus celebrated his *ovatio* by hiding out near Thurii, perhaps in the same mountain haunts they had once shared with Spartacus himself. And so small guerrilla-like bands of peasants, herdsmen and slaves were still being quashed by Roman forces in southern Italy in the late sixties BC. One of the most notable examples of a military operation of this kind must be that of the propraetor Caius Octavius, father of Augustus, the first emperor of Rome (Suetonius *Divus Augustus* 3.2, 7.1).

Crassus' chief rival at the time was already popular with the Roman masses – Cnaeus Pompeius Magnus, proud, pompous and pretentious. As a young outsider he had won spectacular victories for the Sullan regime in Sicily and Africa, and more recently in Iberia, for which he was to earn his second triumph. This marble bust (Paris, Musée du Louvre, Ma 999), dated to 70 BC, represents the up-and-coming Pompey. (Fields-Carré Collection)

THE LEGACY OF SPARTACUS

The myth of the hero is not intended to provide us with icons to admire, but is designed to tap into the vein of heroism within ourselves. Myth must lead to imitation or participation, not passive contemplation, and there is no doubting that Spartacus' determination to win freedom remains as vividly alive today as when his rebellion began. Before the final battle in Stanley Kubrick's epic film *Spartacus* (1960), Crassus tells his gathered officers that his campaign was 'to kill the legend of Spartacus'. In this he was anything but victorious. Spartacus the gladiator was to conquer death and become a myth, an icon of so many scattered and fiercely held hopes.

Usually individuals who figure in history do so because another individual chooses to recount their deeds for posterity. Remembrance is a real and valued form of immortality. Homer immortalized Achilles, as did Virgil for Aeneas, Plato, along with the unpretentious Xenophon, preserved the memory of Sokrates. Caesar naturally took care of his own reputation. But what of Spartacus?

The war against Spartacus was commonly ridiculed and despised at first as merely a matter of gladiators and slaves. Take Florus, for instance, who viewed the rebellion not so much as a monumental struggle for freedom but as a disgraceful undertaking, perpetrated by slaves and led by gladiators, 'the former men of the humblest, the latter men of the worst, class' (*Epitome* 3.20.2). Cicero, a contemporary of Spartacus, once sarcastically referred to a troupe of gladiators as 'impressive, noble, and magnificent' (*Pro Sestio* 134), and was equally scathing about the rebels. Like others of the landowning elite of the time, Cicero viewed Spartacus and those who followed him as sinister insurgents who deserved their fate and who were to be despised as servile people (e.g. *Philippics* 3.21, 4.15, 13.22).

Many of those like Cicero, because of their property interests, tended to be dismissive of the terrible threat Spartacus posed, thinking he would best be forgotten or at least consigned to a small, albeit nightmarish, footnote in the pages of Roman history. The next generation of Romans would be comforted by the thought that Spartacus had taken his place as one of Rome's canonical foes of the past, ranking alongside Hannibal no less, a professional butcher turned outlaw murderer who once threatened the very stability of the Roman ruling order, but had been reduced to a nursery-rhyme bogeyman, a name with which to hush children. Thus, in the polished metal of Horace, Spartacus is chronicled in the line, 'nor Capua's rival strength, nor the fierceness of Spartacus' (*Epodes* 16.5), and again in the lines, 'and wine, that knew the Marsian war, if roving Spartacus had spared a single jar' (*Carmina* 3.14.18-20). And so the

Marx's attention had been drawn to Spartacus by two significant events of his own time, namely the American Crisis, as the civil war was referred to in Europe, and Giuseppe Garibaldi (1807–82), the romantic rebel who was engaged in liberating Sicily and southern Italy from foreign domination. This is his bust in the public garden at the foot of Torre di Federico II°, Enna. (Fields-Carré Collection)

sources on the Spartacan rebellion were not only written by those who owned and hated slaves, but consists of no more than a few passages in Livy, Plutarch, Appian and Florus, less than 4,000 words all told. It seems the whole episode was so humiliating that the less said about it the better. The one exception seemed to have been Sallust.

So Spartacus was too menacing a figure for the Romans to consider a worthy opponent let alone someone worth remembering. Besides he was a slave, gladiator, and rebel, someone who had no business running around being an epic-style hero. However, later generations and cultures would not share this dismissive attitude.

In 1769, twenty years before the fall of the Bastille to the Parisian masses, Voltaire made one of the first specific references to Spartacus in the context of the justification of armed resistance to unjust oppression. In words that would later be echoed in the American Declaration of Independence, Voltaire referred to the rebellion led by Spartacus as 'a just war, indeed the only just war in history' (*Correspondance générale* 461–63, Letter 283, 5.4.1769). As leader of the *Philosophes*, Voltaire's battle cry, which he sometimes used instead of his signature on letters, was '*Écrasez l'infâme!*', 'Crush the infamous!' The Infamous, to him, were those who exercised intolerance and persecution, bigotry, unfair privilege, believed in superstitions, and pursued the empty folly of war. At the time, the so-called Age of Reason, men who were not themselves slaves and had never been oppressed or downtrodden let alone slaves, in other words the well-meaning intellectuals of the day, used the image of the armed rebel slave Spartacus to think about, debate, and promote their own visions of liberty for the freeborn citizens of the newly risen nation-states.

Yet the most striking example of this socio-political phenomenon must be that furnished by Saint Domingue, the French colony that occupied the western part of the Caribbean island of Hispaniola, where rebel slaves and freedmen led by Toussaint L'Ouverture were able to achieve revolutionary freedom by creating a new state fully independent from European domination. A self-educated slave freed shortly before the uprising in 1791, the utterly extraordinary Toussaint joined the black rebellion to liberate the slaves and became its organizational genius. He had read Caesar's *commentarii*, for instance, which had given him some idea of politics and the military art and the connection between them. First defeating the Spanish, and then siding with them to trounce the British, Toussaint finally forced the French to the negotiating table, and thus Haiti, as it was now called, became the first independent black state outside Africa. In 1807, only three years after Haitian independence, the British (and Americans) ended their Atlantic slave trade. Toussaint himself, however, was not to enjoy the fruits of his labours. Treacherously seized and bundled off to France bound like a common criminal, he was to die miserably in a dungeon at Fort-de-Joux high in the Jura Mountains.

It was Karl Marx (1818–83) who brought Spartacus into the centre stage of Roman history, and it was the October Revolution that elevated him into a conscious revolutionary leader with a definite social programme. From that date history took him up, never to let him go. Revolution, says Marx, is the locomotive of history. Even in its neatest sense, 'revolutionary war' refers to the conquest of political power by the use of armed force. If it fails, it routinely becomes, in the jargon of victory, a 'revolt' or a 'rebellion'. Revolution is the source of legal right, but rebellion is a disorder promoted by a group of dissatisfied persons in order to grab, from those in power, both the political sinecures and the economic advantages. The common outcome is no more than a change of hands in the dividing up of prerogatives and perks. Yet as a fully developed concept revolution is a relatively recent phenomenon largely because it is so closely associated with two aspects of modernity – industrialism and imperialism. In every cult there is an element of the untrue and the irrational. In the case of Spartacus, that element is the identification of his rebellion with a conscious attempt at social revolution. Before Spartacus joined the pantheon of revolutionary heroes (or entered into the consumer marketplace, for that matter), he was a slave, a gladiator, a rebel and an inspirational leader.

François Dominique Toussaint L'Ouverture (c. 1744-1803), Haitian patriot and martyr, the 'black Spartacus' who led his people to freedom and independence. Taking heart from the French Revolution, the concepts of *Liberté, Égalité, Fraternité* were manifest in Toussaint's political make-up. Little known in the Anglo-Saxon world, his valiant life and tragic death are the topic of one of Wordsworth's finest sonnets. (Ancient Art & Architecture)

The Roman slave wars, which belong to the second and first centuries BC, probably reflect the big changes going on in the Roman economy and of course society at the time. Certainly these three wars show a massive explosion of slave discontent, but they were not revolutionary mass movements in any sense, the oppressed slaves and free proletariat fighting for their own political space in civil society as it were. Marx explained and predicted all social conflicts were enduring class wars, but it was Lenin who actually developed the idea of a class struggle in antiquity between slave and master – subsequently repeated by Stalin but, ironically, a view not always shared by Marx. Yet of great significance is the fact that no one marched under the banner 'down with slavery' during these wars, on the contrary they were rebellions against individual masters or rebellions by individuals who no longer wanted to be enslaved. In truth, the have-not slaves and proletariat did not rise up to get their share.

In the United States the left-wing novelist Howard Fast, who was imprisoned for his political views, saw Spartacus as the affirmation of man's ability in all eras to resist dehumanization. Greatly encouraged by the writings of Rosa Luxemburg, who had very definite views about freedom, the underlying theme of Fast's 1951 novel *Spartacus* is straightforward, namely that no tyranny, regardless of its power, can ultimately prevail over the force of man's passion for freedom.

Using the little that was known about Spartacus as a basis, even going so far as to teach himself Latin (pity for him the main surviving sources were written in Greek), Howard Fast moulded the gladiator rebel into a mythical hero, a messianic figure engaged in an epic revolutionary struggle to overthrow Rome in order to restore a legendary Golden Age of primitive tribal communism said to have existed in some distant epoch prior to the advent of human exploitation. The modern reader has a developed, scientific view of history, that is to say, we are concerned above all with what actually happened. The story of the Golden Age, a very early and almost universal myth of a lost paradise, when people lived in humble communities with no technology, no art or culture, and no war, was never intended to be historical. For Fast, however, strict adherence to the known historical facts was less important than the timeless moral truth that was implicit in the legend of

On April Fool's Day 1865, Marx's eldest daughter, Jenny, presented her father with a survey asking him his likes and dislikes; favourite food (fish), favourite colour (red), etc. To the question about his heroes, Marx replied 'Spartacus and Kepler'. Yet the philosopher's admiration for the gladiator was a modern sentiment; freedom for him entailed release from commercial labour. (Ancient Art & Architecture)

Spartacus. A myth, after all, does not impart factual information, but is primarily a guide to individual behaviour – it explores our desires, our fears, our longings, and provides a narrative that reminds us what it means to be human. It is not yet out of date. Yet because most of us no longer use myth, Occidental modernity being the child of reason, many of us have lost all sense of what it is.

Compared with Fast's upbeat novel, where Spartacus is the embodiment of the love of life however awful life is, Arthur Koestler's novel takes a rather more melancholic approach. Koestler, who was born in Budapest in 1905, had been an active member of the Communist Party and had fought in the Spanish Civil War, being captured by Franco's rebels at one point and imprisoned under sentence of death. He was disillusioned and embittered by the show trials and left the *Kommunistische Partei Deutschlands* (or KPD, Communist Party of Germany), the successor of the *Spartakusbund*.

His novel, *The Gladiators*, which was written at the time his comrades were being senselessly purged, is about how revolutions turn bad. Man's inability to unite is divinely ordained and inevitable, and thus Spartacus is portrayed as being forced by circumstances to sell out. A grammarian and a rhetorician called Zozimos is given a cynical speech:

> And I tell you, it is dangerous to combine so much power in the fist, and so many lofty reasons in the head, of one single person. In the beginning the head will always order the fist to strike from lofty reasons; later on the fist strikes of its own accord and the head supplies the lofty reasons afterwards; and the person does not even notice the difference. That's human nature my lad. Many a man has started out a friend of the people and ended up as a tyrant; but history gives not a single example of a man starting out as a tyrant and ending up as a friend of the people. Therefore I tell you again: there is nothing so dangerous as a dictator who means well. (*The Gladiators*, 1999, p. 204)

In other words, the end result was always the same, namely an autocratic, centralized government, headed up by a ruthless dictator. The dictator, making a mockery of elementary human rights, had to be obeyed, no matter what he told somebody to do. As with all dictatorships, it was only all right for those at the top. But Spartacus had too much compassion for his followers to take such a route, so he dooms his revolution to certain defeat. The failure of a revolution so often derives as much from the weakness and mistakes of the revolutionaries as it does from the strength of their opponent. We leave to the political pundits of cynical wisdom the dubious pleasure of pointing out (from the hindsight of the 20th-century Soviet experience) that perennial chestnut that 'revolutions always eat up their children'.

Fast may have believed in the nobility of the human spirit, not so James Leslie Mitchell. Mitchell found a natural attraction to the story of the Spartacan rebellion and, writing under his Scottish pseudonym of 'Lewis

Grassic Gibbon', he produced *Spartacus* in 1933 at the height of the Great Depression. As a Diffusionist, Mitchell believed civilization was a blight, overtaking originally free and happy humanity from the Egyptian pyramid-builders onwards, bringing to people who were already living full and imaginative lives settlement, culture, as well as property, compulsion, war, tyranny, religion, and mental enslavement. The novel is a telling indictment of men's inhumanity to those over whom they have total control.

Since the consensus of our ancient authors is that Spartacus died in battle, his elevation to the cross can have no purpose other than to evoke comparison with that other famous freedom fighter, the Nazarene. Slain by oppressors, his death thus acquires an aura of sanctity and he himself becomes a sort of proto-Christ, a secular Messiah. In this respect it is interesting to note that Gibbon's novel begins and ends on the same note: 'It was the Springtime in Italy, a hundred years before the crucifixion of Christ'. In death the gaunt and bearded Che Guevara bore an uncanny resemblance to a sacrificed Christ, which helped create an image of him as a martyr and prophet. Like Spartacus, Che Guevara became a more potent symbol in death than he had ever been in life. Men (and women, for that matter) do not die when their life and example can serve as a guide to others.

For James Leslie Mitchell (Lewis Grassic Gibbon), a lifelong follower of Marx and a successful historian of early civilization, Spartacus allowed him to focus on his fiercely held beliefs in the nature of society, the freedom of the individual, and the inevitable collapse of civilization. He published *Spartacus* in 1933, two years before his sudden death at the age of 34. (The Grassic Gibbon Centre)

The intelligentsia of the Soviet Union had a near-obsession with Spartacus as a 'world revolutionary figure'. The two decades between 1933 and 1953 formed a period when the collective political thinking of the Soviet intelligentsia, following leaden hints in directives issued by Comrade Stalin, was dominated by the doctrine that the Spartacan rebellion had been a class struggle between the oppressed and their oppressors, a conflict between the 'slave-owner class' and 'politically-aware slaves'. Then along came Joseph Vogt and a band of fellow German academics flaunting an anti-Soviet banner. Obviously finding fault with the Stalinist view that Spartacus led a revolutionary armed struggle that overturned the domination of the class system of the time, Vogt and his nationalist chums were keen to present a more sympathetic view of slavery; though the institution was morally wrong, was it really that bad after all? Such conceptualizations fitted in nicely with the contemporary climate of Cold-War rhetoric and helped combat the communist use of the Spartacan rebellion as a means of ennobling and encouraging the class struggle against modern capitalism. On his side of the Iron Curtain Vogt turned away from the nastier aspects of slavery by highlighting the practice of manumission, wet-nursing, patriarchal relationships, and the like.

Standing against this anti-communist-cum-humanistic approach was Moses Finley who announced, in his typically uncompromising fashion, that in the final analysis the slave was a piece of movable property and even if granted certain privileges these were unilateral grants from an individual master and not a right that recognized the slave as a human being. To use the happiness of some to offset the misery of others (surely the vast majority) was pointless.

A GUIDE TO PRIMARY SOURCES

The most important written sources for any reconstruction of the Spartacan rebellion are the accounts by the Roman historian Sallust, the Greek biographer Plutarch, and the Greek historian Appian. Plutarch's *Life of Crassus* (8–11) provides the following skeleton of events:

- The garrison of Capua is overcome.
- The praetor Glaber (Plutarch simply calls him Clodius) with 3,000 troops is defeated.
- Varinius enters the story: his legate Furius is routed (with 2,000 men) as is his fellow praetor Cossinius (surprised by Spartacus), then Varinius himself.
- Spartacus takes Varinius' horse. Meanwhile Gellius, one of the consuls, falls on a contingent (Plutarch specifically calls it the German contingent) from the slave army and destroys it.
- Lentulus, the other consul, is in turn defeated by Spartacus, who sets off for the Alps, where he confronts and routs Cassius (with 10,000 men) the governor of Gallia Cisalpina.
- Crassus, decimating the survivors of Mummius' legions, establishes firm leadership while Spartacus heads south for Lucania and the sea; bargains with Cilician pirates but is betrayed by them.
- Spartacus establishes himself in Bruttium; Crassus traps the slave army with a fortified trench; dissent in the slave camp.
- Crassus begins to fear the return of Pompey. Meanwhile, Spartacus escapes with one-third of his army through Crassus' barrier on a snowy, stormy night. The slaves, internally divided and weakened by desertion, are beaten once (Plutarch mentions the force under Castus and Gannicus, the latter he calls Caius Canicius) and head for the mountains of Petelia.
- Spartacus turns on his pursuers and routs them, seriously wounding the quaestor Scrofa (*Skrophas* in Plutarch's Greek).
- The final battle in Lucania; Spartacus is cut down while trying to reach and kill Crassus.

By using additions and modifications from Sallust and Appian, a fuller, more vibrant picture of the rebellion is feasible. Sallust's *Historiae*, for instance, provides an insight into the relevance of the rebellion to the machinations of the Senate and its internal politics, volatile at best especially so when we consider the clash of egos that were Crassus and Pompey. Unfortunately for us, however, the *Historiae*, composed some 35 years after the event, and thus arguably the most original source on the rebellion, remains only in tantalizing fragments. But then Appian's *Bellum civilia*, his books dealing with the civil wars of the Republic, are intact and offer us (1.116–121) some dramatic details:

- The occupation of Mount Vesuvius.
- The names of Oenomaus and Crixus.
- The sacrifice of Roman prisoners to the *manes* of dead Crixus.
- The near-attack on Rome (not in Plutarch) inexplicably abandoned.

Moreover, Appian's description of the breakout from Crassus' trap in Bruttium is full and vigorous. His description of the final battle, which cost Spartacus his own life, is also vivid. There again, before the concluding climax Plutarch has Spartacus sacrifice his superb white stallion. Of course the two Greek writers composed their accounts about two centuries after the rebellion occurred, while all three came from the privileged elites of their day. Sallust was a Roman senator retired from active politics, Plutarch and Appian wealthy Greek aristocrats with close political ties to the imperial establishment, and naturally none of them had much sympathy for slaves.

Indeed, we must remember that these writers viewed the Spartacan rebellion as nothing more than a hiccup in the grand scheme of things. Not one account was written by a slave or a former slave, and because the rebels have left no statements of their aspirations and intentions, their view of events must remain irrecoverable. Thus it has to be understood that the information we have comes from non-slave sources, men who rationalized the behaviour of the rebel slaves in their own way, and, as in all things human, from afar events are imagined more straightforward and less intertwined, yet everything looks different close to.

Only our three main authors are listed in the pages that follow. Further details about these authors, and information about other sources, is most conveniently available in *The Oxford Classical Dictionary* (3rd edition). In the following notes 'Penguin' denotes Penguin Classics, and 'Loeb' denotes Loeb Classical Library. The Loeb editions, which are published by Harvard University Press, display an English translation of a text next to the original language.

APPIAN (b. AD 95)

Appian (Appianus) was an Alexandrian Greek who rose to high office in his native city, and appears to have practised law in Rome, where he pleaded cases before the emperors Hadrian and Antoninus Pius. He composed his *Roman Affairs* (*Romaika*) sometime during the reign of Antoninus Pius, at the height of the period that Edward Gibbon aptly labelled 'the golden age of the Antonines'. Appian's target audience was the cultured Greek-speaking privileged elite of the eastern Mediterranean, who had long been not merely affected by Roman rule, but also deeply involved with its workings. Some of its members had already become Roman senators and even consuls, while many more, like Appian himself, had benefited from imperial patronage. But although Rome had established a secure world order, it remained a foreign power, its history generally little understood or appreciated by men who had been brought up on the Greek classics and did not subscribe to quite the same values as their political masters.

Twenty-four books in length, Appian's account of Roman history is essentially a narrative of conquest and struggle, and therefore a narrative of war. His fundamental aim is to paint a clear picture of the relationship of the Romans to the various nations whom they brought under their sway. This leads him to break up his narrative in such a way that each book deals with the interaction of Rome and a particular ethnic group. Nonetheless, he follows a fairly clear chronological scheme, placing the books in the order in which the various peoples first clashed with the Romans. There is a Loeb translation of what survives of Appian's work as a whole, while a Penguin edition entitled *The Civil Wars* admirably covers the period from 133 BC down to 35 BC, that is, from the time when Tiberius Gracchus was clubbed to death by his political opponents to the terrible civil conflicts following the murder of Caesar by his so-called friends, and thus includes the chapters dealing with the Spartacan rebellion.

PLUTARCH (*c.* AD 46–120)

From Chaironeia in Boiotia, the hugely learned and prolific Plutarch (Lucius [?] Mestrius Plutarchus) was an aristocratic Greek who moved in the cultured Roman circles of his day, and may have held some imperial posts under the emperors Trajan and Hadrian. He also served as a member of the college of priests at Delphi. Greece was then a comfortable, demilitarized backwater of the Roman empire and Athens itself, where he studied philosophy as a young man, a self-satisfied university town and cultural centre. No matter they had been dead for centuries, Athens was still the city of Plato and Aristotle, and for any philosophically and academically inclined student it had status, class, and a reputation that other places of learning could never equal.

His *Parallel Lives* (*Bioi paralleloi*) is an extremely useful source for Roman (and Greek) history, as he collected much detail and various traditions. However, Plutarch can be fairly uncritical. His main aim is to moralize about the nature of the man, this keen interest in individual psychology being coupled with an equally keen eye (as Shakespeare was to appreciate) for a dramatic situation. Yet it should be said that Plutarch does make a fair stab in some of the *Lives*, which were written in pairs of Greeks and Romans of similar eminence and then a comparison between the two, at producing some sort of history. Thus, for instance, Agesilaos is compared with Pompey and Nikias with Crassus. The *Lives*, of which there are 23 pairs and four that have been left unpaired, are available in various Penguin and Loeb volumes.

SALLUST (86–*c.* 35 BC)

Sallust (Caius Sallustius Crispus), who held various public offices in Rome and later a governorship in Africa, was a partisan of Caesar and an opponent of Pompey. He was born in Amiternum, a provincial town in the Sabine highlands of central Italy, and during the early years of his political career he became involved with the *populares*, among whom Caesar was the most prominent. A *popularis* was an aristocratic populist who tended to bypass the Senate by enlisting the support of the tribunes of the people and through them of the people at large. He passed through the junior magistrates of a senatorial career, becoming a quaestor around 55 BC, and, in 52 BC, he was elected as one of the tribunes of the people. Two years later he was expelled from the Senate by the censors for alleged immorality; much that was said about him by his enemies was mere malicious gossip. A year or so later, however, the influence of Caesar enabled him to be elected to a second quaestorship and to re-enter the Senate.

Sallust crossed the Rubicon with Caesar, and during the years 49 to 45 BC he loyally served him as an officer in various campaigns of the civil war, was elected praetor, and was installed by the dictator as governor of Africa Nova, a province just formed from the kingdom of the pro-Pompeian Iuba of Numidia. Sallust is said to have fleeced the provincials ignominiously and to have been saved from conviction only by the good grace of his patron, to whom he apparently gave a sizeable backhander. Certainly he did very well by Caesar, owning a grand villa at Tibur (Tivoli) and a splendid park at Rome, the celebrated *horti Sallustiani*, which the historian lavishly embellished from his own purse.

A recently resurfaced section of the Via Appia in Rome, photographed in the 1950s. Built on a monumental scale, Roman roads combined practical utility with visually impressive statements of power. They also provided direct, well-maintained routes along which the legions could move with ease.
(Library of Congress)

As a historian Sallust is best known for his two surviving monographs, the *Bellum Iugurthinum*, which describes the war between Rome and the Numidian king Iugurtha from 112 to 105 BC, and the *Bellum Catilinae*, which describes the unsuccessful rebellion against the Roman Republic in 63 BC. In the late forties BC, having set aside the sword for the pen after the death of Caesar, Sallust also wrote a continuous history of Rome in five books, which covered the events from the rebellion of Marcus Aemilius Lepidus in 78 BC at least down to the year 67 BC if not 60 BC, the year the opportunistic coalition between Pompey, Crassus, and Caesar, the so-called first triumvirate, was formed. It is known that the Spartacan rebellion was included, but unfortunately only a few set speeches and letters and a quantity of short narrative fragments of the *Historiae* survive. There are all sorts of reasons why these particular bits and pieces rather than any others survive the centuries, amongst them pure chance.

Sallust may have proved to be a poor soldier, but he was certainly to become famous as a writer of influential style. Keen to illustrate to his readership the decline and corruption of the Roman state, which he ascribes to the refinement and riches created by the wars of the second century BC, Sallust writes in a highly individual and somewhat artificial style, mostly in short, terse sentences, packed full of ideas that he seems impatient to express. He is fond of antithesis, imitating here the Greek style of Thucydides, whom he greatly admired, but avoids symmetry and smoothness, even to the point of abruptness.

Another of Sanesi's illustrations for Giovagnoli's *Spartaco*, this time depicting Spartacus sacrificing his horse before the final showdown with Crassus. Frequently reprinted after its initial publication, as well as translated into many other languages, this historical masterpiece also provided the basis for the first cinematic portrayals of Spartacus, produced in the fledgling nation of Italy just prior to World War I. (Reproduced from R. Giovagnoli, *Spartaco*, Rome, 1874)

BIBLIOGRAPHY

Adcock, F.E., *Marcus Crassus: Millionaire* (Cambridge: Heffer & Sons, 1966)

Bradley, K.R., *Slavery and Rebellion in the Roman World, 140 BC – 70 BC* (Bloomington & Indianapolis: Indiana University Press, 1989, 1998)

Brown, S., *Spartacus* (Nottingham: Warhammer Historical Wargames, 2004)

Brunt, P.A. *Italian Manpower 225 BC – AD 14* (Oxford: Oxford University Press, 1971, 1987)

Brunt, P.A. *The Fall of the Roman Republic and Related Essays* (Oxford: Clarendon Press, 1988)

Cohen, G.A. *Karl Marx's Theory of History: A Defence* (Oxford: Clarendon Press, 1978)

Gabba, E. (trans. P.J. Cuff) *Republican Rome: The Army and Allies* (Oxford: Blackwell, 1973)

Garnsey, P.D.A. and Saller, R.P. *The Roman Empire: Economy, Society and Culture* (London: Duckworth, 1987)

Grant, M. *Gladiators* (London: Penguin, 1967, 2000)

Greene, K. *The Archaeology of the Roman Economy* (Berkeley & Los Angeles: University of California Press, 1986, 1990)

Fields, N. *The Roman Army: The Civil Wars 88–31 BC* (Oxford: Osprey – Battle Orders 34, 2008)

Finley, M.I. *Ancient Slavery and Modern Ideology* (Princeton, NJ: Markus Weiner, 1980, 1998)

Finley, M.I. *The Ancient Economy* (London: University of California Press, 1999, 2nd ed.)

Harris, W.V. 'Spartacus', in M.C. Carnes (ed.), *Past Imperfect: History according to the Movies* (New York: Henry Holt, 1996), pp. 40–43

Hopkins, K. *Conquerors and Slaves* (Cambridge: Cambridge University Press, 1978)

James, C.L.R. *The Black Jacobins* (London: Penguin, 1938, 2001)

Katzenberger, E. (ed.) *First World, Ha Ha Ha! The Zapatista Challenge* (San Francisco: City Light Books, 1995)

Marshall, B.A. *Crassus: A Political Biography* (Amsterdam: Hakkert, 1976)

Rice Holmes, T. *The Roman Republic* (Oxford: Oxford University Press, 1923)

Rubinsohn, W.Z. (trans. J.G. Griffith) *Spartacus' Uprising and Soviet Historical Writing* (Oxford: Oxbow Books, 1983)

Shaw, B.D. 'Bandits in the Roman Empire', *Past & Present*, 105 (1984), pp. 3–52

Shaw, B.D. (ed.) *Spartacus and the Slave Wars: A Brief History with Documents* (Boston & New York: Bedford/St Martin's Press, 2001)

Stockton, D.L. *Cicero: A Political Biography* (Oxford: Oxford University Press, 1971)

Sullivan, J.P. (ed.) 'Marxism and the Classics', *Arethusa*, 8:1 (1975), pp. 5–225

Trow, M.J. *Spartacus: The Myth and the Man* (Stroud: Sutton, 2006)

Urbainczyk, T. *Spartacus* (London: Bristol Classical Press, 2004)

Vogt, J. (trans. T.E.J. Wiedemann) *Ancient Slavery and the Ideal of Man* (Oxford: Blackwell, 1974)

Ward, A.M. *Marcus Crassus and the Late Republic* (Columbia and London: University of Missouri Press, 1977)

Welch, K. 'The Roman arena in late republican Italy: A new interpretation', *Journal of Roman Archaeology*, 7 (1994), pp. 59–80

Winkler, M.M. *Spartacus: Film and History* (Oxford: Blackwell, 2007)

Wisdom, S. *Gladiators 100 BC – AD 200* (Oxford: Osprey – Warrior 39, 2001)

Yavetz, Z. *Slaves and Slavery in Ancient Rome* (Oxford: Transaction Books, 1988)

Ziegler, K. 'Die Herkunft des Spartacus', *Hermes*, 83 (1955), pp. 248–50

GLOSSARY AND ABBREVIATIONS

Aedile — Annually elected junior magistrate (two plebeian and two curule or patrician) responsible for public works and games.

As/asses — Copper coin, originally worth 1/10th of *denarius* (q.v.), but retariffed at 16 to the *denarius* at the time of Gracchi.

Aquila/aquilae — 'Eagle' – standard of *legio* (q.v.).

Aquilifer/aquiliferi — 'Eagle-bearer' – standard-bearer who carried *aquila* (q.v.).

Capite censi — 'Head count' – Roman citizens owing insufficient property to qualify for military service.

Centurio/centuriones — Officer in command of *centuria* (q.v.).

Centuria/centuriae — Sub-unit of *cohors* (q.v.).

Cohors/cohortes — Standard tactical unit of *legio* (q.v.).

Contubernium — 'Tentful' – mess-unit of eight legionaries, ten per *centuria* (q.v.).

Denarius/denarii — 'Ten as piece' – silver coin, now worth 16 *asses* (q.v.).

Dilectus — 'Choosing' – levying of troops.

Dolabra/dolabrae — Pickaxe.

Eques/equites — Member of equestrian order.

Furca/furcae — T-shaped pole carried by legionaries.

Gladius/gladii — Cut-and-thrust sword carried by legionaries.

Impedimenta — Baggage animals.

Legio/legiones — Principal unit of Roman army.

Lorica hamata — Mail armour.

Magister pecoris — Head herdsman.

Manipulus/manipuli — 'Handful' – tactical unit of manipular legion of middle Republic.

Mille passus — 'One-thousand paces' – Roman mile (1.48km).

Munus/munera — 'Obligation' – gladiatorial fight.

Pala/palae — Spade.

Patera/paterae — Bronze mess tin.

Passus/passuum — 'One-pace' – 5 Roman feet (1.48m).

Pilum/pila — Principal throwing weapon of legionaries.

Pilum muralis — Wooden stake for marching camp defences.

Pugio/pugiones — Dagger carried by legionaries.

Scutum/scuta — Shield carried by legionaries.

Sesterce/sestertii — Brass coin worth 1/4 of *denarius* (q.v.).

Signum/signa — Standard of *centuria* (q.v.).

Talent — Fixed Greek weight of silver equivalent to 60 *minae* (Attic-Euboic *tálanton* = 26.2kg, Aiginetan *tálanton* = 43.6kg), the *mina* being a unit of weight equivalent to 100 Attic *drachmae* or 70 Aiginetan *drachmae*.

Trulleus — Bronze cooking pot.

Quaestor — Annually elected junior magistrate principally responsible for financial matters.

Vilicus/vilici — Bailiff.

Abbreviations

AE — L'Année Épigraphique (Paris, 1888–)

CIL — T. Mommsen et al., *Corpus Inscriptionum Latinarum* (Berlin, 1862–)

ILS — H. Dessau, *Inscriptiones Latinae Selectae* (Berlin, 1892–1916)

MMR II — T.R.S. Broughton, *The Magistrates of the Roman Republic*, Vol. II (New York, 1952)

INDEX

Figures in **bold** refer to illustrations.